Home of the Brave
AN AMERICAN HISTORY BOOK FOR KIDS

Home *of the* BRAVE

AN AMERICAN HISTORY BOOK FOR KIDS

15 Immigrants Who Shaped U.S. History

Brooke Khan

Illustrations by Iratxe Lopez de Munain

ROCKRIDGE PRESS

Interior and Cover Designer: William Mack
Art Producer: Sue Bischofberger
Editor: Mary Colgan
Production Manager: Oriana Siska
Production Editor: Erum Khan

Illustrations © Iratxe Lopez de Munain/Illustration Inc., 2019

ISBN: Print 978-1-64152-780-4 | eBook 978-1-64152-781-1

For Sam and Micah

Contents

Introduction

Immigration is the process of leaving one country to live in another. Throughout history, immigrants have moved all over the world. They bring with them new ideas, rich cultures, and different traditions. Because of immigration, the world is a more connected place.

We can learn a lot from the experiences of immigrants. Leaving home to live in a new place is challenging. The immigrants you will learn about in this book worked hard to achieve their dreams. They had to use determination to overcome incredible obstacles. Can you imagine leaving your home and moving to a new country? Take a moment to think about how different it would be. You might have to speak a different language, eat different foods, and make new friends. There would be so many new things to discover.

The 15 immigrants featured on the following pages were chosen for their dedication to making the world a better place and their commitment to hard work. Their accomplishments made a difference and will continue to have an impact on future generations of Americans.

As you read about each immigrant, think about where they came from, the obstacles they overcame to reach their goals, and how their achievements affected the lives of others. Then think about how you can apply their different experiences to your own goals and dreams. Dive into the stories, connect with each fascinating life, and see what stays with you after you turn the last page. Let these 15 amazing people inspire you!

ENGINEER'S COAT

LEVI STRA
SAN FRANCISCO

LEVI STRAUSS & CO
SAN FRANCISCO

& CO

TION COAT

Levi
STRAUSS
1829–1902

Levi Strauss (born Loeb Strauss) was a German-American businessman who completely changed the clothing industry when he started manufacturing a new line of heavy-duty denim work pants.

Loeb Strauss was born in the German state of Bavaria in 1829. His parents, Hirsch and Rebecca Strauss, had one other child together, Loeb's older sister Fanny. Hirsch had four other children from a previous marriage, making Loeb the youngest of six children.

Hirsch supported the large Strauss family by selling fabrics and other small household items as a traveling peddler. In 1845, tragedy struck when Hirsch died of tuberculosis. Rebecca was left alone to support herself and the three children still living at home.

With few opportunities in Bavaria, Rebecca decided to move the family to New York City. There, two of Loeb's brothers had already built their own dry goods business. Soon after arriving in America, Loeb began working with his brothers and learning English. He was

18 years old. He applied for US citizenship and changed his name to Levi—a new name to match his new life.

When news of the California Gold Rush reached the East Coast, Levi and his brothers began preparing to open a branch of their dry goods business out west. The Strauss brothers were eager to take advantage of the new business opportunity and decided Levi should run the West Coast operations. Levi began making arrangements to travel across the country.

In 1853, the quickest route from New York City to San Francisco was to go south by ship, cross through Panama in Central America, and then travel north along the coast. Although dangerous and expensive, the trip would take only six weeks. A land journey across the country could take six months.

Not wanting to waste any time, Levi boarded a steamship in New York and sailed to Central America. Upon arrival in Panama, he began his trek through the jungle, traveling by train, boat, and mule to reach the Pacific Ocean. A second steamship took him the rest of the way up the coast of North America.

Levi was 23 when he arrived in the fast-growing port city of San Francisco. With the support of his family in New York, Levi quickly set up a dry goods whole-saler business. The Strauss brothers on the East Coast shipped barrels of blankets, clothing, fabric, umbrellas, and other necessary household items to Levi in San Francisco. Levi then sold the goods to his customers, small shops that provided needed items to the growing population of the West.

By the late 1850s, Levi's sister Fanny, her husband, and their young son had also moved to San Francisco. Levi began working with his brother-in-law and changed the name of his business to Levi Strauss and Co. to indicate that he now had a partner.

Levi was known for his fairness and honesty in business dealings and was becoming one of the most successful merchants in the western United States. Retail stores from Montana to Hawaii sold his merchandise.

Nearly 20 years after arriving in San Francisco and becoming a successful businessman, Levi was approached by one of his customers with a very clever idea. Jacob Davis, a tailor from Nevada, had come up with a way to reinforce work pants to make them tougher. This was something miners had requested for years. Jacob figured out that if he added rivets (small metal pins) to the points on the pants that got the most strain, the pants would be stronger and last longer.

Levi was impressed by Jacob's idea and agreed to join him in business. Together they applied for a patent, a license from the government that would protect their invention. In 1873 the patent was approved, and Levi's blue jeans were born.

Originally the pants were called overalls, and Levi's design was perfect for all types of laborers. Up until that time, men had worn uncomfortable overalls on top of their regular clothing as an added layer of protection while they worked. Everything changed with the arrival of Levi's riveted jeans. Made from an all-cotton fabric called denim, Levi's jeans were comfortable, affordable, and, with the addition of the rivets, tough.

The first batch of Levi's jeans were called simply "XX." They were made with denim and sewn with orange or yellow thread. Belt loops hadn't been invented yet, so the jeans had a strap and loop in the back of the waistband so the size could be adjusted. The first pairs of jeans also had buttons for suspenders, and, of course, the rivets.

By the 1880s, Levi's blue jeans were extremely popular. To keep up with the demand, Levi leased factory space in San Francisco and hired women to sew larger quantities of the popular "XX" jeans.

Levi's patent expired in 1890. Right away other manufacturers started producing denim jeans with rivets. To let customers know they were buying an original pair of Levi's, an image was added to the back of each pair of jeans. The image was printed on a small leather patch and showed two horses trying to rip apart a pair of jeans, to indicate the pants' strength and quality. Still used today, the image of the two horses reminds customers that their high-quality jeans are genuine Levi's.

As a leading businessman in San Francisco, Levi joined organizations that connected him with other successful merchants and executives. Levi understood

> **"I DO NOT THINK LARGE FORTUNES CAUSE HAPPINESS TO THEIR OWNERS, FOR IMMEDIATELY THOSE WHO POSSESS THEM BECOME SLAVES TO THEIR WEALTH."**

the importance of supporting western businesses and contributed to a number of industry associations, including the San Francisco Board of Trade and San Francisco Chamber of Commerce.

Levi was also passionate about supporting local charities. To show his commitment to young people and education, Levi donated the money for 21 scholarships to the University of California at Berkeley in 1897. The Levi Strauss scholarships are still in place today.

Levi never got married and never had children. Instead, he built his life around his business. When he died in 1902, the news made headlines across the country. He had earned people's respect, for his achievements and for who he was as a businessman.

Levi Strauss and Co. was left to Levi's four nephews, and it is still a family business today.

Surprisingly, Levi never wore a pair of jeans in his life. In the late 1800s, successful businessmen wore expensive suits, silk ties, and sometimes even a top hat to show their place in society. Jeans were considered work wear for men who had jobs that required heavy labor.

Even though he didn't wear the jeans he helped create, Levi manufactured a product that changed the clothing industry forever. Levi's jeans are still popular today and continue to be a symbol of inventiveness. Through hard work and determination, Levi Strauss created an American product that is famous through-out the world.

EXPLORE MORE! Learn more about Levi Strauss & Co. Browse through all the different styles of jeans, or find out how Levi's supports important social issues at www.LeviStrauss.com.

TIPS FOR YOU! Kids can be inventors, too! Are you an inventor? Use everyday items to create something new.

Mary Harris
JONES
c. 1837–1930

Mary Harris Jones was an Irish-American teacher, dressmaker, and activist. As a labor organizer, Mary fought tirelessly for America's hardest workers.

Mary Harris was born in Cork, Ireland, around the year 1837. When she was a child, Ireland was controlled by England, its powerful neighbor. Many of Mary's family members fought for Irish independence and were killed for resisting British control.

In addition to political difficulties, Ireland was also going through an extreme food shortage. More than half of the Irish potato crop was destroyed by disease, and over a million people died from starvation. To keep the family safe, Mary's father made the decision to leave Ireland and move to America.

Soon after arriving in the United States, Mary's family moved to Toronto, Canada. There, her father found work in railroad construction. Living in the safety of Canada, Mary went to school and learned the skills of dressmaking. She also had a desire to become a teacher, a goal that was considered quite ambitious for an Irish immigrant.

Mary moved back to the United States to start her career as a teacher. Her first position didn't last long. After teaching at a school in Michigan for just eight months, she quit. She then moved to Chicago and found work as a dressmaker. Although Mary "preferred sewing to bossing little children," she gave teaching one more chance when she moved to Memphis, Tennessee.

While living in Tennessee, Mary met George Jones. They were married in 1831 and had four children. George was an iron molder and member of the Iron Molders Union. The Iron Molders Union was made up of craftsmen who worked with metal to make products. Union members joined together to fight against low wages and unsafe working conditions. Mary became interested in the process and learned as much as she could about labor unions from George.

In 1867, a deadly virus known as yellow fever swept through Memphis. Thousands of people were affected. Tragically, Mary lost George and her four children to the disease. Heartbroken and alone, Mary moved back to Chicago.

Using her dressmaking skills, Mary found work as a seamstress. Sewing for the rich people of Chicago gave Mary an opportunity to observe luxury and wealth every day. It upset her to see the huge contrast between the rich and the poor.

Tragedy struck again when Mary lost everything in the Great Chicago Fire of 1871. The fire burned for three days, killing 300 people and leaving nearly 100,000 people homeless. Left with nothing, Mary camped at a church until she could find a new place to live.

While staying at the church, Mary spent the evening hours attending Knights of Labor meetings. The Knights of Labor, founded in 1869, was an organization that supported all types of workers in their fight for better working conditions.

Mary decided she wanted to become more involved in the fight for workers' rights and joined the Knights of Labor. At the time, the labor movement in the United States was just beginning. More and more Americans were working in factories, mines, and mills as the economy moved toward industrialization (an increase in the number of industries in a region). As a result, workers were forming unions to fight for better pay, reasonable working hours, and safer working conditions.

Organizations like the Knights of Labor used strikes to bargain with business owners. A strike is when workers refuse to work, which costs the business valuable production time. Using what she had learned from George, along with her own fearless determination, Mary did very well as an activist for the Knights of Labor. She helped organize successful strikes, ran educational meetings, and energized workers with inspiring speeches. People began to see Mary as a champion for the working class, and she was given the nickname "Mother Jones."

Mary continued her work with the Knights of Labor for several more years. In the 1890s she became an organizer for the United Mine Workers and greatly increased the number of members in the organization. Mary also encouraged wives to fight alongside their husbands. Because she believed that justice for workers depended on strong families, she often included wives and children in her events.

Mary wanted to raise awareness of issues involving child labor, so she organized a children's march from the city of Philadelphia to President Theodore Roosevelt's summer home in Long Island, New York. She walked from town to town with boys and girls who had been harmed working in mills and factories. In each new town, they gained attention with rallies and speeches. Soon, Mary's dramatic form of protest made the front page of newspapers.

In 1912, Mary risked her life when she helped coal miners fight for fair pay during the West Virginia Paint Creek–Cabin Creek strike. Mary brought the workers together and organized a march to the steps of West Virginia's capital. The strike dragged on for months, until violence broke out between the miners and mine operators. Members on both sides were killed.

For her participation in the strike, Mary was arrested and charged with conspiracy to commit murder. She was convicted and sentenced to 20 years in prison.

"I ABIDE WHERE THERE IS A FIGHT AGAINST WRONG."

Her prison sentence got national attention and, after reviewing the case, the governor of West Virginia released her.

A year after she was set free in West Virginia, Mary was back in prison. In 1913 she joined striking coal miners in Colorado. The miners were fighting for a work day of eight hours, better pay, and freedom to organize. They also wanted their union to be recognized. Mine owners tried to limit Mary's involvement with the workers and had her removed from the mine property twice. Refusing to leave, Mary was arrested and jailed each time.

The tension continued to rise until armed guards opened fire on the striking workers. Twenty-five people were killed, including eleven children. Mary was outraged by the tragedy and urged members of Congress to take action. As a result, President Roosevelt sent troops to Colorado to bring order back to the situation.

During the following years, Mary participated in strikes all over the country. She also took her labor efforts across the border when she joined Mexican workers in their fight against the crooked actions of the people in power. In 1921 Mary was invited by the Mexican government to attend the Pan-American Federation of Labor meeting due to the positive changes she helped bring about in Mexico.

Mary took part in her last strike in 1924. She traveled to Chicago to support dressmakers in their struggle for better pay and working conditions. Mary, or "Mother Jones," continued to speak out in support of workers' rights until her death in 1930. Thousands of miners attended her funeral to pay their respects to the woman who had worked so hard for them.

A magazine named *Mother Jones*, in honor of Mary Harris Jones, was created in 1976. Inspired by Mary's efforts in the labor movement, the magazine provides readers with serious news stories about important issues, such as politics, the environment, and human rights. *Mother Jones* magazine is still publishing news in print and online, and also has a podcast.

Although she was only five feet tall, Mary was a giant when it came to fighting for workers' rights. She used powerful speeches, dramatic rallies, and public marches to bring attention to the unfair conditions that working-class people faced. Mary devoted her entire life to organized labor efforts and, in the process, became a symbol of protest.

EXPLORE MORE! Did you know that during World War II, women in the United States played essential roles at home and overseas? Look up Rosie the Riveter at www.WomensHistory.org to find out more.

TIPS FOR YOU! It's time for a change! What is something you would like to change? Think of three steps you would need to take to make that change happen. Get started today!

John
MUIR
1838–1914

John Muir was a Scottish-American naturalist and writer who strongly supported preserving America's wilderness. He is often referred to as the "Father of the National Park System," and his passionate efforts led to the protection of millions of acres of land in the United States.

John Muir was born in the small coastal town of Dunbar, Scotland, in 1838. His parents were Daniel and Ann Muir, and he had seven brothers and sisters. As a young boy, John loved adventure, and he always had someone to join him for a day of exploration. Whether he was roaming through fields or listening to songbirds, John was happiest when he was outdoors.

When he was 11 years old, John learned that his family would be leaving Scotland in search of a better life in a country far away. This was exciting and sur-prising news to John. Soon after, he and his family boarded a ship and set sail across the Atlantic Ocean.

After almost seven weeks at sea, John landed in America, the place he would now call home.

In 1849, the Muir family settled on a wild patch of farmland in the state of Wisconsin. Building the farm from scratch was hard work. Because he spent long hours plowing the fields and feeding the livestock, John was no longer able to attend school. When he could sneak away from the watchful eye of his strict father, John loved to explore the woods, prairies, and lakes that surrounded the family farm.

Besides being an enthusiastic outdoorsman, John was a talented inventor and wood carver. At a young age, he was able to turn scraps of wood and steel into tools, machines, and clocks, and he even displayed several of his inventions at the Wisconsin State Fair. Eventually, John made plans to leave the farm and pursue his passions.

At the age of 23, John left home to study at the University of Wisconsin. While in college, John's appreciation for the environment grew stronger. After taking science courses for several years, he made the decision to begin one of his greatest adventures. He was committed to exploring the world on foot, so he walked from Indiana to the Gulf of Mexico—more than 1,000 miles of rough land. Along the way, John kept a detailed journal filled with sketches and descriptions of the different types of plants and animals he found along the way.

After arriving at the Gulf of Mexico, John sailed to Cuba, Panama, and up the West Coast of the United

States. In 1868, he landed in San Francisco and decided to make the state of California his permanent home. John immediately fell in love with the Sierra Nevada Mountains. For the next four years, he herded sheep and explored the natural treasures of Yosemite Valley.

Yosemite sits at the center of the Sierra Nevada mountain range and is filled with rivers, waterfalls, lakes, meadows, mountains, and forests. John found comfort living alone in the peace of the wilderness. As he did when he was young, he spent many hours exploring the variety of nature surrounding his new home.

The immense beauty of Yosemite inspired John. While living there, he started writing and publishing articles about the natural wonders he encountered. His vivid descriptions of the ancient giant sequoias, great granite domes, and sparkling glacier lakes jumped off the page and fascinated all types of readers. They became as enthusiastic about the environment as John was.

John wanted to protect the delicate wilderness of Yosemite Valley, so he began campaigning for action by Congress in Washington. He urged the government to adopt policies that would help conserve and protect native lands. Focusing on the destruction of mountain meadows and forests, John wrote a series of popular articles that got attention across the nation. These articles and the reaction to them inspired lawmakers to create Yosemite National Park in 1890.

As an energetic supporter of land preservation, John believed that national parks should be off-limits to industries and development. He wanted natural spaces set aside for people to enjoy. At his urging, Congress passed actions to create Sequoia National Park in California, Mount Rainier National Park in Washington, and Grand Canyon National Park in Arizona.

John's passionate conservation efforts attracted the attention of President Theodore Roosevelt. President Roosevelt traveled to Yosemite, was instantly mesmerized by the natural beauty, and made huge progress to start the nation's first conservation programs. As president, Roosevelt signed the paperwork to create five national parks, 18 national monuments, and 150 national forests. Over 230 million acres of land were placed under the protection of the federal government, making them safe from destruction by industries.

Wanting to settle down and start a family, John moved to Oakland, California. There, he met and married Louisa Strentzel. In 1880, the couple settled down in a small town outside the city, and John helped manage the Strentzel family fruit ranch. Not long after, their family grew with the addition of two daughters.

Even though John no longer lived in the wilds of Yosemite, he continued to write books and express his passion for conservation. Over the next several years, John wrote more than 300 articles and 10 books.

"IN EVERY WALK WITH NATURE, ONE RECEIVES FAR MORE THAN HE SEEKS."

It was soon clear that John was the nation's leader in a movement that was changing the way people thought about nature.

In 1892, at the age of 54, John helped create the Sierra Club, an organization dedicated to protecting the nation's wilderness. As president, John made the club's mission very clear: He wanted people to be able to explore, enjoy, and protect the planet.

Wanting a passport so he could travel to other countries, John applied for and was granted US citizenship in April 1903.

John traveled the world, turning his adventures into articles and books for people who were interested in reading about nature. He visited every continent except Antarctica. He even explored the wild rain forests of the Amazon jungle.

After a long life filled with adventure, John lost a battle with pneumonia in 1914. He was 76. Despite his death, John's memory as a dedicated naturalist and conservationist lives on. His efforts increased people's awareness of nature and inspired activists around the world. His passion for preserving the environment led to important changes in how natural lands in the United States are managed.

The protected wilderness areas that John helped create give people from all over the world the chance to appreciate America's natural beauty. Schools, parks, monuments, wilderness areas, trails, and historic sites have been named for John Muir, honoring his efforts to protect the environment.

For John, nature was something to be treasured and defended. He saw humans as part of the natural world, not the center of it. He believed all living things were part of something bigger, and he lived his entire life according to that belief.

From the soggy wetlands of Scotland to the magnificent mountains of California, John tackled one adventure after another. His detailed descriptions of the world around him will continue to inspire and educate others for years to come. More importantly, John Muir started an environmental movement that works to preserve America's natural treasures for future generations.

EXPLORE MORE! Become a National Park Service Web Ranger! Play games, design a ranger station, hike virtual trails, and learn more about America's National Park Service. Go to www.nps.gov/webrangers.

TIPS FOR YOU! Start your own nature journal! Go outside and record your observations. Sketch or write about what you see and hear. Everything you put in your journal is up to you. Be creative, and make it your own!

Albert
EINSTEIN
1879–1955

A lbert Einstein was a German-American scientist who developed groundbreaking theories in the field of physics. He completely changed scientific thinking and is considered to be one of the greatest scientists who ever lived.

Albert Einstein was born in a small German town near the Danube River in 1879. Raised in a middle-class Jewish family, Albert and his younger sister, Maria, had a fairly traditional childhood. Albert's father, Hermann, worked in the new field of electronics, and his mother, Pauline, ran the household.

When Albert was still a small child, his family moved to the larger city of Munich, Germany. Although Hermann worked long hours, he enjoyed discussing science and math with his young son. Pauline was a strong woman who pushed her children to stay focused and work hard to be successful.

As a young child, Albert was slow to learn how to talk. This worried his parents for the first few years of his life. Eventually, Albert began speaking normally and grew into a determined young boy with a strong interest in learning. He was constantly thinking and loved to solve riddles. He also had a passion for classical music and started playing the violin at six years old.

Although he was a gifted student, Albert didn't enjoy school. He didn't like teachers telling him what to do and had a hard time following the rules. Preferring to study alone, Albert spent hours working on math problems. His teachers believed he might have a learning disability, but soon enough it was clear that Albert was extremely intelligent. Often outsmarting everyone in the classroom, Albert regularly earned high marks in math and science.

As the years went by, Albert became more and more focused on trying to understand the world around him. When his father gave him a magnetic compass as a gift, Albert was instantly fascinated and wanted to figure out how it worked. His passion for learning was intense.

When Albert was a teenager, his father's job forced the family to move to Italy. But Albert's parents insisted that Albert stay in Germany with a relative so he could finish high school. At the time, all German boys had to serve in the military at age 16. Albert had no interest in joining the military, so he made the life-changing decision to fake sickness, drop out of school, and surprise his parents in Italy.

Because he failed to finish high school, it was difficult for Albert to find a university that would accept him. Eventually, he scored high enough marks on the entrance exams to get into a school in Zurich, Switzerland. Albert loved the freedom that studying at a higher level gave him, and he did extremely well in physics, the branch of science that deals with matter, energy, motion, and force.

While attending school in Zurich, Albert met Mileva Marić. Mileva was a physics student from Serbia, a small country in Southeastern Europe. She was four years older than Albert, extremely smart, and also passionate about science. Connected by their shared interest in physics, the couple fell deeply in love.

Albert's parents didn't approve of the relationship because Albert and Mileva had such different backgrounds. This made Albert hesitate to ask Mileva to marry him. But Mileva was soon pregnant, and their first child, a daughter, was born.

At the time, it wasn't acceptable in society for a couple to have a child before marriage. Having a child without being married would ruin Albert's chances of finding work, so he made the difficult decision to give up his baby daughter. Not long after, Albert graduated from university and got a job reviewing patents for the Swiss government.

After receiving approval from his parents, Albert finally married Mileva in 1903. A year later, their first son was born. Although he had a wife and child, Albert stayed committed to working on his scientific theories. He was convinced his hard work would eventually pay off and spent most of his free time dedicated to science instead of his family.

Thankfully, Albert's commitment to his work paid off. In 1905, he published four articles in the most well-known physics journals. His theories were ground-breaking and changed the course of science forever.

First, Albert proposed that light was made up of tiny particles called photons. Next, his theory of relativity explained the link between space and time. Finally, Albert defined the relationship between matter and energy with his famous equation $E=mc^2$.

Albert's work dealt with major questions and common problems in mathematics, and made a huge contribution to the foundation of modern physics. His theories changed the way the world thought of space, time, matter, and energy. As his work became more and more accepted by others, Albert's reputation as an important scientist grew. His family was also growing. Mileva gave birth to their second son in 1910.

As a leader in the field of physics, Albert was now able to begin a career as a university teacher. By 1914, he had been teaching for several years and living in Switzerland for most of his adult life. At that point, Albert decided to move back to Germany to teach at the University of Berlin.

Albert's success in the field of physics had a high price. His family life was falling apart. In 1919, his

"IMAGINATION IS MORE IMPORTANT THAN KNOWLEDGE."

relationship with Mileva was under too much strain to continue, and their marriage ended. Later that year, Albert married his cousin Elsa Löwenthal.

In 1921, while living in Germany, Albert was awarded the Nobel Prize in physics. Winning one of the world's most respected awards instantly made him famous. Albert spent the next several years lecturing all over the world, presenting his discoveries. He was given numerous honors for his brilliant work and became a symbol for the promise of science.

As Albert's career as a famous scientist was rising, the country he called home was in bad shape. Almost destroyed after World War I, Germany was experiencing great uncertainty and confusion. These unstable conditions were perfect for the rise of the Nazi Party, led by Adolf Hitler. Promising to return Germany to greatness, Hitler became the leader of the country in 1933.

According to Hitler, Jewish people were the cause of Germany's problems. New German laws forced Jewish citizens out of their jobs and identified them as a lesser race. As a result, Jewish people in Germany were no longer safe. Albert became a target for the Nazis and, fearing for his life, he set sail for America. He would never return.

Albert settled in the state of New Jersey, working as a researcher for Princeton University. Because he was no longer teaching classes, he had more time to work on his scientific theories. Albert was comfortable with life in America, and he became a US citizen in 1940.

As Albert worked to explain the laws of physics, Hitler was preparing to invade other European countries. In 1939, Germany invaded Poland, starting World War II. Albert was outraged by Hitler's actions and wrote a letter to President Franklin Roosevelt to express his concerns.

Even though Albert was against war and violence, he knew Hitler had to be stopped. He urged President Roosevelt to begin developing the atomic bomb, the only weapon that could end the horrible war. Albert was never personally involved in building the atomic bomb, but his theories on energy and mass were important in creating it.

While the war was being fought in most of the world, Albert continued to work on his scientific theories. He had ideas about time travel, black holes, and the creation of the universe. When the war ended in 1945, Albert spoke out against developing more nuclear weapons. He believed countries needed to work together to avoid war and maintain peace.

In his later years, Albert campaigned for civil rights and an end to segregation in the United States. He could still remember the discrimination he faced in Germany. He joined organizations to fight for equality and was passionate about protecting human freedom. Albert believed all people should be respected, no matter what their race or religion is.

In 1955, at the age of 76, Albert died in a Princeton hospital. He was often considered the first "celebrity scientist." With his death, he left behind an incredible body of work, including theories that laid the foundation for modern science.

Albert Einstein is still an inspiration to young scientists everywhere. He was a man with an endless imagination, who worked hard and was determined to succeed despite the hardships he faced. He changed how humans understand the world, and he will always be remembered for his passion, dedication, and enthusiasm for science.

EXPLORE MORE! Learn more about the importance and history of the Nobel Prize. Visit www.NobelPrize.org to watch interviews with past winners, learn about the prize categories, and play games created by Nobel Laureates.

TIPS FOR YOU! Would you like to create rain in a jar, change the color of leaves, or turn a pumpkin into a volcano? Find the instructions for a bunch of experiments you can do at home at www.ScienceFun.org.

Mabel Ping-Hua
LEE
1896–1966

Mabel Ping-Hua Lee was a Chinese-American activist and reformer. (A reformer is a person who works to change something in order to make it better.) She was dedicated to improving the rights of women and played an important role in the fight to get women the right to vote. Her story of unshakable determination inspires women of all backgrounds to set their sights high and achieve their dreams.

Mabel Ping-Hua Lee was born in 1896 in Canton, a busy port city in Southern China. She was the only child born to her deeply religious Christian parents. Not long after Mabel's fourth birthday, her father moved to the United States in search of work and better opportunities. Mabel stayed in China with her mother and grandmother.

When Mabel was old enough to attend school, she was enrolled at a Chinese Christian academy. Curious and excited to learn, she did extremely well in school. Mabel took classes in English, and she picked up the language quickly. She didn't know it at the time, but her knowledge of English would soon become very useful.

In 1905, Mabel and her family left China, traveled halfway around the world, and joined her father in New York City. Mabel quickly got used to her new life in America. She was a focused and talented student, and earned many awards and honors for her schoolwork.

In addition to her dedication to learning, Mabel felt strongly about women's rights. At the time, the United States didn't allow women to vote. Suffrage, which means the right to vote in elections, was available only to men. In the late 1800s, the women's suffrage movement began. It was a campaign led by activists and reformers who worked to get voting rights for women. Mabel was passionate about creating change and unafraid of opposition. She soon joined the fight for women's rights.

Eager to make a difference, Mabel helped lead a parade for women's voting rights in New York City in 1912. Riding a horse at the head of the parade, Mabel moved through the crowded streets of New York City, trying to build up support for the important cause. More than 10,000 people attended the parade. Mabel became a well-known figure in the suffrage movement in New York, a remarkable achievement for a 16-year-old girl.

Mabel's willingness to speak out about improving the lives of women got the attention of top New York newspapers. Although she was only a high school student, she was featured in several New York publications and called a leader for women's rights.

Mabel continued her fight for equality at Barnard College in New York City. Wasting little time, she joined the Chinese Student Association and wrote essays arguing for the rights of women. The demands of college life meant that Mabel had to work extra hard to balance her schoolwork and her dedication to the women's movement.

Somehow, Mabel managed to find the time to write, prepare, and deliver speeches to the Chinese-American community, urging them to participate in the fight for women. Mabel believed that a successful democracy (a system of government set up by the people) depends on the votes of everyone, including women.

During her time at Barnard College, the 19th amendment to the US Constitution was passed, giving women the right to vote. Although this was a huge achievement for the women's rights movement, the amendment only applied to women who were citizens of the United States.

Mabel wasn't allowed to become a US citizen due to the Chinese Exclusion Act. This was a law passed by Congress in 1882 that limited Chinese immigration and prevented Chinese people from becoming US citizens. Because she was a Chinese citizen, Mabel was denied the right to vote, a right she had worked so hard to achieve.

Even though she couldn't become a US citizen and take part in the election process, Mabel continued to push for equal rights.

A determined young woman with big goals, Mabel became the first woman to enter the PhD program at Columbia University. While working on her PhD in economics, Mabel served as a leader of the Columbia Chinese Club. She was also the associate editor of *The Chinese Students' Monthly*, where she continued to write and publish articles on the need for equality between women and men. In 1921, she graduated with a PhD in economic history.

Mabel had never lost sight of her strong Chinese roots and thought about returning to China after graduation. She had connections with new leaders in China and felt passionate about her home country. She also believed the future success of China depended on its commitment to women's equality. But before Mabel made the decision to leave New York, a tragic turn of events caused her to change her plans.

In 1924, Mabel's father died of a heart attack, leaving Mabel to care for her mother. Mabel's father had been an important member of the Chinese community. Before his sudden death, he had been the pastor and leader of the First Chinese Baptist Church in Chinatown.

Mabel vowed to continue what her father had built for the Chinatown neighborhood. Just five weeks after he passed away, she took on his role as leader of the important community church. She gave up her dreams of creating change in China to focus on creating change in New York City instead.

Mabel's passion for equality was as strong now as it had ever been. She was determined to make the church a place where all members of the community could get help. To make sure that the church would continue to go on, Mabel made several improvements.

She organized a fundraiser to buy a new building, and moved the church and the community center into a more modern space. She also focused on providing social services that would give support to members of the community. With Mabel's hard work and determination, the church began offering English classes, opened a medical clinic, and started enrolling students in its new kindergarten program.

Mabel continued to serve the people of Chinatown until her death in 1966. She was 70 years old. Mabel never married, instead devoting most of her life to the Chinese residents of New York City. The First Chinese Baptist Church is still standing today, and continues the work Mabel started, offering support and assistance programs to members of the community.

In honor of Mabel's dedication to the people of New York City, the United States Post Office in Chinatown was renamed the Mabel Lee Memorial Post Office in 2018.

Although she is rarely mentioned today, Mabel Ping-Hua Lee was an important figure in the women's rights movement. She saw the connection between women's suffrage and the needs of a strong nation. Her fierce determination and commitment to women's rights are an inspiration to those still fighting for equality.

EXPLORE MORE! Learn about another important activist for women's rights, Sojourner Truth. After escaping from slavery in 1826, Sojourner Truth spent the rest of her life devoted to fighting for the rights of all people. Read the book *Who Was Sojourner Truth?* by Yona Zeldis McDonough to discover more about her inspiring story.

TIPS FOR YOU! Take a stroll online through the hallways of the National Women's History Museum. You can explore documents from the women's rights campaign. You can also watch videos and read articles about the history of the suffrage movement and how it changed over time. Go to www.WomensHistory.org.

Maya
DEREN
1917–1961

Maya Deren (born Eleanora Derenkowsky) was a
Ukrainian-American filmmaker, lecturer, and
writer. Her original and creative techniques changed
the film industry and inspired artists everywhere to be
bold and take risks.

Eleanora Derenkowsky was born in the capital
city of Kiev, Ukraine, in 1917. She was the only child
born to her Jewish parents, Marie and Solomon
Derenkowsky.

When Eleanora was still a small child, the Jewish
citizens of Ukraine were suffering horrific acts of
racism. Anti-Jewish pogroms (organized massacres)
were occurring throughout the country. In 1922, with
their lives in danger, Marie and Solomon made the
decision to take young Eleanora and escape to the
safety of the United States.

After a long trip across the Atlantic Ocean, Eleanora
and her family landed in America. They settled in
Syracuse, New York. Eleanora's father, a doctor,

found work at a local psychiatric hospital. In 1928, the Derenkowskys became US citizens and shortened their last name to Deren.

Eleanora attended elementary school and high school in Syracuse, and was an excellent student. She was very intelligent and did so well in school she was allowed to skip ahead two grade levels and graduate early.

In 1930, at the young age of 13, Eleanora moved to Europe to attend the International School of Geneva founded by the League of Nations. She spent the next three years in Switzerland pursuing her passion for the arts, studying language, going to plays, and writing poetry. Eleanora was extremely creative and took advantage of every artistic opportunity that came her way.

When she returned to New York in 1933, Eleanora entered Syracuse University to study journalism and political science. During her time in college, she met and married another Syracuse student, Gregory Bardacke. The couple moved to New York City, and Eleanora finished her degree at nearby New York University.

Married life was difficult for Eleanora and Gregory, and after two years of trying to make it work, the young couple divorced in 1938. Eleanora went on to attend Smith College in Massachusetts, where she earned a master's degree in English literature.

After finishing graduate school, Eleanora got a job doing secretarial work for the great dancer Katherine Dunham. Crisscrossing the country with the famous performer gave Eleanora a chance to learn more about

"THE WAY BACK IS ALWAYS SHORTER."

dance and movement, something she would put to use in later years.

At the end of the dance tour, Eleanora settled in Los Angeles to pursue a career in writing. She published poetry, essays, and newspaper articles, but her creative instincts were pulling her in a different direction.

In 1942, Eleanora met and married Alexander Hammid, a motion picture photographer. It didn't take long for the couple to join forces and become well known in the world of film. As she began a new career in motion pictures, Eleanora legally changed her name to Maya in 1943.

The couple shot their first film, *Meshes of the Afternoon*, in their home. Alexander was behind the camera and Maya played the lead role. Because they were working on their own and not for a movie company, Maya and Alexander had the freedom to explore fresh ideas and new approaches to filmmaking. *Meshes of the Afternoon* was filled with unusual camera angles, creative editing, and slow-motion scenes, taking viewers on a wild ride.

After the success of their film, Maya and Alexander moved to New York City. They rented a small studio apartment and used the space to continue their artistic work. The techniques that Maya and Alexander were developing were like nothing anyone had ever seen, and a new movement in film was starting to take shape. Although they made a great team as filmmakers, their marriage was not as successful and they eventually got divorced.

By 1945, Maya had created two more groundbreaking films, and her influence as a filmmaker was starting to grow. Maya was determined to share her art with the world, so she did something that had never been done before. She rented a small theater in New York City to show three of her latest films. Her bold action inspired other filmmakers to start doing the same thing.

To highlight the beauty and power of moving pictures, many of Maya's films don't include any spoken words. Maya wasn't afraid to take risks. She used sudden cuts between scenes, played with time and space, and used dramatic body movements to bring the stories in her films to life.

In 1946, Maya was the first filmmaker to win the Guggenheim Foundation Fellowship, an award for outstanding creative ability in the arts. Maya used the grant money from the award to travel to Haiti, where she filmed native rituals and dance. Her Haitian film was never finished, but she used her background in journalism to publish a study of the native Haitian religion.

Maya's bold techniques and dedication to her work inspired other filmmakers to follow in her footsteps. To promote young artists, she set up the Creative Film

Foundation in 1955, which provided money for new and independent filmmakers.

In 1960, Maya married Teiji Ito, a young Japanese musician. Teiji was a talented composer and created soundtracks for two of Maya's films. In 1961, only a year after they were married, Maya died suddenly from a brain hemorrhage at the age of 44.

Although Maya died at a fairly young age, her contributions to the film industry were huge. In addition to her work as a filmmaker, Maya lectured, taught, and wrote about her craft. In 1985, the American Film Institute created the Maya Deren Award to honor the contributions and importance of her film work.

Maya's imaginative work continues to have an impact on filmmakers everywhere, and her films are studied at the most respected schools around the world. Maya Deren inspires artists to take risks and be bold. She saw film as a serious art form and paved the way for future filmmakers who want to explore new forms of expression.

EXPLORE MORE! Go behind the scenes of the magical world of film with the *Children's Book of Cinema*. Learn everything you ever wanted to know about movies!

TIPS FOR YOU! Have a silent conversation! Try "talking" to someone without using any words. Exaggerate your facial expressions and use big gestures to express yourself.

I. M.
PEI
1917–2019

I eoh Ming (I. M.) Pei was a Chinese-American architect who set the standard for modern architecture. Pei's projects featured clean lines (meaning the design kept things simple and wasn't crowded with lots of details), bold patterns, and thoughtful use of natural surroundings. His award-winning work pushed design into new directions.

I. M. Pei was born in Canton, China, in 1917. The oldest of four children, I. M. was raised in a traditional Chinese family. His father was a well-known banker, and his mother was a devoted Buddhist and skilled flute player.

As a child, I. M. moved with his family to the larger Chinese cities of Hong Kong and Shanghai. While walking through the busy streets of Shanghai with his uncle, I. M. was fascinated by the magnificent skyscrapers that towered above him. He spent hours sketching them, including even the smallest details of the Shanghai skyline.

At the age of 17, I. M. left China to attend college in the United States. He enrolled in the engineering program at the University of Pennsylvania.

I. M. still had the fascination for buildings that had taken hold of him when he was just a boy. After learning more about architecture, I. M. realized that he didn't have to be a gifted artist to pursue his passion. He decided to transfer schools and focus on learning the practice of designing and constructing buildings. Four years later, he graduated with a bachelor's degree in architecture from the Massachusetts Institute of Technology.

I. M. continued his study of architecture at the Harvard University Graduate School of Design. While at Harvard, I. M. had the opportunity to work with the famous German architect Walter Gropius. Gropius taught I. M. to focus on designing useful spaces with clean lines. I. M. would never forget what he was taught and used what he learned throughout his career.

During his time in graduate school I. M. met and married Eileen Loo, another architecture student. They made a home for themselves in New York City and became parents to four children.

In 1948, I. M. began his career working for a well-known real estate development company. As director of architecture, I. M. worked on a series of major projects across the country. The boy who was amazed by the steel giants in Shanghai now had the opportunity to bring his sketches to life.

One of I. M.'s first important projects was the Mile High Center in Denver, Colorado. I. M. designed four buildings, 22 stories high, that were connected to each other. This enormous complex was the first of its kind, and it included a hotel, a parking structure, a department store, and open space for people to enjoy. With this project, I. M. had proved he was a key player in the field of architecture.

In 1954, 17 years after arriving in America, I. M. became a US citizen. A year later, I. M. left the security of his company job and set up his own firm, I. M. Pei & Associates.

Over the next several decades, I. M. refined his work and became known for his strong and clear architectural style. Remembering his days at Harvard, I. M. focused on using simple materials and uncomplicated shapes to serve as the building blocks for his modern designs.

The first project to highlight his style of architecture was the National Center for Atmospheric Research in the foothills of Boulder, Colorado. Inspired by Native American cliff dwellings, I. M. combined art and architecture to create a building that would blend in with the natural surroundings. His thoughtful use of concrete and modern design captured the public's attention and made him the leading contender to design a bold new building in Washington, DC.

The East Building of the National Gallery of Art in Washington, DC, was one of I. M.'s greatest challenges.

The plot of land that the building would sit on had an odd shape, making it difficult to construct a useful space. In addition, I. M. had to create something that would last a long time and blend in well with other buildings in an area that displayed great achievements in architecture. With a bit of creativity and a lot of skill, I. M. designed a building with one of the most unusual shapes in a city filled with famous monuments.

When President John F. Kennedy died in 1963, an architect needed to be found to design his presidential library. Presidential libraries and museums promote understanding of the presidency, protect historical documents, and allow the public to view interesting presidential materials. Kennedy's widow, Jacqueline Kennedy Onassis, considered many well-known architects but decided on I. M. to preserve her husband's memory. He did so with a nine-story concrete and glass masterpiece on the waterfront near Boston. Completion of the Kennedy Library put I. M. in the national spotlight.

Although he had many early successes, I. M. also experienced his fair share of setbacks. The John Hancock Tower in Boston, for example, had many problems. Before the building was completed, glass windows in the 60-story skyscraper began popping out and falling to the sidewalk below. The tower also had other construction problems, ran into financial

"A LASTING ARCHITECTURE HAS TO HAVE ROOTS."

troubles, and was delayed for various reasons. I. M. considered the entire project a disaster.

In 1989, I. M. set off to work on several major international projects. For one of his most famous designs, I. M. used simple lines and shapes to bring new life to the entrance of the Louvre Museum in Paris. He created a 70-foot-tall glass pyramid that attracts visitors into the centuries-old French landmark. Because it was constructed of glass, the new entrance also allowed light through to the reception area below. The design of the pyramid, along with the technology needed to make it work, made the Louvre one of I. M.'s greatest accomplishments.

Not long after making his mark in Paris, I. M. returned to his home country to design the Bank of China Tower in Hong Kong. I. M. had his work cut out for him. He had to create a tower that was tall enough to meet the demands of the client, but strong enough to stand up to the tremendous winds of a typhoon. After four long years, the building was finally completed. Covered in glass, the award-winning 70-story skyscraper is now one of the most recognizable sights in Hong Kong.

In the later years of his career, I. M. continued to design impressive buildings, including the Rock and Roll Hall of Fame in Cleveland, Ohio. He also completed projects on a remote mountain in Japan, in the beautiful gardens of his youth in China, and on a man-made island in the scorching desert of the Middle East. The boy who was fascinated by the towers in Shanghai had designed his own magnificent buildings all over the world.

Over his career, I. M. won many awards for his work, including recognition from the Smithsonian Institution and the National Endowment for the Arts. In 1983, he won the Pritzker Prize, architecture's top award. I. M. used the prize money from the Pritzker to start a scholarship for Chinese students so they could study architecture in the United States. I. M. also earned one of the highest civilian awards in the United States, the Presidential Medal of Freedom, for his strong moral character and celebrated achievements in architecture. The Presidential Medal of Freedom, established by President John F. Kennedy in 1963, recognizes individuals who have made outstanding contributions to the United States and the world. It is one of the highest civilian awards in the United States.

In 2019, I. M. Pei died in New York City at the age of 102. He had dedicated more than 60 years of his life to perfecting his craft. I. M. pushed the limits of modern architecture by using the power of simple shapes, focusing on usefulness, and considering a building's natural surroundings. He was a visionary designer with great creativity and imagination who produced designs no one had ever seen before. His work will surely inspire young architects for years to come.

~~~~~~

EXPLORE MORE! Research more amazing achievements in architecture! Check out the following five famous buildings: the Burj Khalifa in Dubai, the Lotus Temple in Delhi, the Cybertecture Egg in Mumbai, the Blue Planet in Denmark, and Metropol Parasol in Seville. Can you find five more?

TIPS FOR YOU! Unleash your inner architect! Build a toothpick structure, construct a sandcastle, or design a new layout for your bedroom. The sky is the limit! Check out www.ArchKidecture.org for more ideas and inspiration.

Elie
WIESEL
1928–2016

E lie Wiesel was a Romanian-American Holocaust survivor, novelist, human rights activist, and winner of the Nobel Peace Prize. In his famous book *Night*, he exposed the horrors of the Holocaust, recording the events to ensure that such a tragedy would never happen again. Elie dedicated his life to fighting for human rights and promoting world peace.

Elie Wiesel was born in the town of Sighet, in Romania, in 1928. He was raised in a Jewish family and had two older sisters and one younger sister. Elie's parents, Shlomo and Sarah Wiesel, owned a grocery store in their small town.

At the age of three, Elie began attending a local Jewish school. In addition to speaking Yiddish, a dialect of German, he learned to speak Hebrew, the language used for prayer and religious study in many Jewish communities.

As Elie grew older, he became more interested in the Jewish religion. He studied religious texts on his own, and he spent a great deal of time talking about Judaism with the caretaker of his local synagogue.

At the start of World War II, Elie's town of Sighet was turned over to Hungary by German Nazis, led by dictator Adolf Hitler. In 1942, the government of Hungary ordered all Jewish people who couldn't prove they were Hungarian citizens to be transferred to concentration camps in Poland and killed.

Although they were afraid of the Hungarian government, the Jewish people of Sighet didn't think the rest of the world would allow such atrocities to be committed. They also believed the end of the war was near. Daily life went on, and Elie celebrated his bar mitzvah in 1942. A bar mitzvah is a religious ceremony and celebration that takes place when a Jewish boy turns 13 years old.

In 1944, five years after the start of World War II, the threats against the Jewish people living in Sighet became real when German soldiers arrived. The Jewish citizens of Sighet were stripped of all their freedoms. Their shops were closed, their homes were raided, and they were forced to wear yellow stars on their clothing, which identified them as Jewish. After losing everything, they were also forced to live in ghettos, which were crowded sections of the city set aside for Jewish residents.

Living in ghettos was difficult. Windows facing the street were sealed closed, and barbed wire was put up around the perimeter. Even though the conditions were miserable, Elie and his family believed they would be safe until the end of the war. Although they were under the command of the German army, they found comfort living together as a family.

Everything changed in 1944. The Wiesel family was one of the last Jewish families in Sighet to be forced onto a crowded cattle car and shipped to a concentration camp. The concentration camps were large prisons where the Nazis held and killed their prisoners. Elie and his family were sent to Auschwitz, a concentration camp in southern Poland.

The trip to Auschwitz lasted four miserable days. The doors of the train car were nailed shut, making the air difficult to breathe and the heat almost unbearable. When they arrived in Auschwitz, the men and women were immediately separated. Elie never saw his mother or younger sister again.

To stay with his father, Elie lied about his age. He was only 15 years old, but he said he was 18 when asked by the German guards. After being judged healthy enough to work, Elie and his father had identification numbers tattooed on their arms. They were then sent to do forced labor.

Elie and his father survived together in Auschwitz for eight brutal months. They were forced to work from sunrise to sunset each day and were given only a small piece of bread and a cup of soup to live on. Elie and his father suffered beatings, experienced extreme hunger, and witnessed horrible acts of cruelty.

When the prisoners weren't being forced to work, they were being forced to march. In the winter of 1945, Elie, his father, and thousands of other prisoners were forced to march hundreds of miles to another concentration camp in Germany. Prison marches usually occurred in freezing temperatures. Very little food was given to the prisoners, and they weren't given a chance to rest. These marches were known as death marches because thousands of prisoners died from the cold, lack of food, and exhaustion.

The grueling march was too much for Elie's father. Shortly after the prisoners arrived at the Buchenwald concentration camp, Shlomo Wiesel died of dysentery, starvation, and exhaustion. Nothing mattered to Elie after he lost his father. Now orphaned and alone, he was sent to live in the children's section of the prison.

Three months later, American armed forces arrived at the camp. Elie and the thousands of other prisoners were finally free. Not long after, Elie went into the hospital for stomach sickness. After he recovered, he and other orphans were taken to France, where he lived for the next several years.

In 1947, Elie learned that his older sisters had survived the war, and they were all reunited. A year later he enrolled in Sorbonne University in Paris, where he studied literature, philosophy, and psychology. Eventually he found work as a journalist, tutor, and Hebrew teacher.

Elie vowed that he would never write about his experiences in the Nazi prison camps because he didn't believe he could accurately describe the horror. In 1955, while he was working as a journalist in New York, Elie was hit by a taxi. His injuries were serious, and he was in the hospital for months. During his recovery, he concentrated on his writing.

After 10 years of silence, Elie realized it was important for him to tell his story, so he began writing down his experiences. His book *Night*, which describes his experiences in the concentration camps, was published in 1956. The book tells the story of a teenage boy who lost everything he loved, including his family, friends, and faith in God. By sharing his memories, Elie made sure that the horror millions of innocent people suffered would never be forgotten.

After the publication of *Night*, Elie continued to write novels, essays, and plays. Most of his writing centered on the subject that would always haunt him—the Holocaust. In 1963, with no place he could call home, Elie applied to become a citizen of the United States.

In 1969, Elie married Marion Rose, who had also survived the Holocaust. They settled in New York and had a son, Shlomo Elisha, who was born in 1972. After the birth of his son, Elie began teaching Jewish studies at the City University of New York. Four years later, he accepted a teaching position at Boston University.

In addition to writing and teaching, Elie traveled the world to speak about human rights. He came to be seen as a messenger of peace for humanity and was awarded the Nobel Peace Prize in 1986. In his acceptance speech, Elie spoke about the importance of keeping the memories of the Holocaust alive.

After witnessing the dark side of humanity, Elie relied on the power of tolerance, learning, and faith to spread awareness of human rights. In 1992, Elie was awarded the Presidential Medal of Freedom for his work speaking out about the Holocaust and other human rights crimes all around the world.

Elie played a leading role in the creation of the United States Holocaust Memorial Museum in Washington, DC. He was one of many influential leaders to give a speech at the opening in 1993. The museum is intended to be a living memorial to the Holocaust, inspiring people around the world to battle hatred, put a stop to genocide (the killing of a group based on race or culture), and support human dignity.

In 2009, Elie traveled with President Barack Obama to visit the site of the Buchenwald concentration camp in Germany. It was important for Elie to share his personal experiences as a Holocaust survivor. After the trip, the president described Elie as someone who raised his voice against hatred and encouraged others to do the same.

Elie Wiesel died in New York in 2016. He was 87 years old. He recorded his personal experiences to expose the horrors of the Holocaust, hoping to prevent similar tragedies in the future. He worked tirelessly as an advocate for human rights, fighting oppression all over the world. A symbol of determination and strength, Elie Wiesel survived a war and dedicated his life to promoting peace.

EXPLORE MORE! Read about the Holocaust from the perspective of a young girl. *Anne Frank: The Diary of A Young Girl* provides a firsthand account of Anne's life while she and her family hid from the Nazis during World War II.

TIPS FOR YOU! Learn more about the Holocaust. Visit the United States Holocaust Memorial Museum in Washington, DC, or go online (www.ushmm.org) to see an extensive collection of historic documents, articles, and photographs.

Madeleine
ALBRIGHT
1937–

Madeleine Albright (born Marie Jana Korbel) is a Czech-American author and former diplomat. As America's first female secretary of state, she was a trailblazer in the field of politics. She was a leader in international relations and set a new standard for women around the world.

Marie Jana Korbel was born in Prague, Czechoslovakia, in 1937. Family members started calling her Madeleine when she was a young girl, and the nickname stuck with her for the rest of her life. Madeleine was the eldest of three children, and her parents were Josef and Anna Korbel. Josef Korbel worked as a diplomat, representing Czechoslovakia in dealings with other countries.

When the Germans invaded Prague in 1939, Madeleine and her family found safety in England. At the end of World War II, the Korbels moved back to Czechoslovakia. Soon, Madeleine's family found themselves packing their belongings once again. The Czech government had been overthrown, and Madeleine's father, who supported democracy, decided it would be best for the family to immigrate to America. Once again, they left their home and moved to another country.

Madeleine, now 11, and her family set sail for the United States. As they approached Ellis Island in the New York Harbor, they were greeted by a majestic symbol of hope and a promise of a better life—the Statue of Liberty.

In 1949, Madeleine's father accepted a teaching position at the University of Denver in Colorado. Like her father, Madeleine was interested in foreign affairs. She founded her high school's international relations club and served as its first president.

Madeleine was an excellent student and earned scholarships to many different colleges. After discussing her options with teachers she respected, Madeleine chose to attend Wellesley College in Massachusetts.

Wellesley College is an all-girls school, and it sparked Madeleine's feminist spirit. Working together in this academic environment encouraged the women of Wellesley to push the limits of what they could achieve. While she was at Wellesley, Madeleine made what she calls the best decision of her life. In 1957, she became a citizen of the United States.

Madeleine spent the summer working as an intern at a newspaper in Colorado. There, she met Joseph Albright, a young journalist from a prominent family. The couple fell in love, and they got married three days after Madeleine graduated from Wellesley.

"WHEN PEOPLE HAVE THE CAPACITY TO CHOOSE, THEY HAVE THE ABILITY TO CHANGE."

The newlyweds lived in Missouri for a short time while Joseph finished his military service for the army. They then moved to Chicago, where Joseph got a job working for a top newspaper. Next it was New York, where Joseph got another newspaper job. In 1961, Madeleine and Joseph's twin daughters were born.

Madeleine was eager to continue her education. She enrolled in the PhD program at Columbia University, focusing on public law and government. When her third daughter was born in 1967, Madeleine found herself juggling the duties of motherhood while trying to keep up with her studies. It was an overwhelming balancing act; she often joked that women can do everything, just not all at the same time.

Like the days of her youth when she wasn't in one place for too long, Madeleine found herself packing again when she, Joseph, and their girls moved to Washington, DC. There, Madeleine organized fundraisers for her daughters' school and served on the local board of education.

During her time living in Washington, Madeleine got her first taste of political life. Ed Muskie, a senator from Maine, asked her to organize a campaign dinner. Impressed with her abilities, Senator Muskie hired

Madeleine to be his assistant. At 39 years old, while raising three daughters and earning a graduate degree, she was about to start a career in politics that would pave the way for future generations of women.

In 1978, President Jimmy Carter hired Madeleine to be a member of the White House staff. She was now working with the most powerful people in the world every day.

While Madeleine was doing well in her new career in politics, she was struggling in her personal life. In 1981, Joseph decided to end their marriage and they got divorced. Madeleine was shocked and shaken. She spent the next 10 years developing her independence and sense of identity as a woman on her own.

When President Carter left office in 1982, Madeleine's time as a White House staff member came to an end. With a PhD in international studies and experience working in politics, Madeleine was hired as a professor at Georgetown University's School of Foreign Services. Georgetown had recently started accepting female students and wanted more women on its faculty. This made Madeleine an excellent choice for the position.

While teaching at Georgetown, Madeleine stayed active in Washington politics. She continued to work on campaigns and became known for her skills in foreign relations. In 1993, Madeleine stepped into a global spotlight. President Bill Clinton selected her to be the United States Ambassador to the United Nations.

The United Nations is an organization of countries from all over the world that agree to work together to solve problems, promote peace, and end wars. As an ambassador at the United Nations, Madeleine found her voice. She was a fierce supporter of American interests in other countries, and she grew America's role in UN operations. As a woman in a room filled with men, Madeleine had to have courage to speak up. She realized that if she remained silent, America wouldn't be represented in worldly affairs.

In 1997, Madeleine made history when President Clinton named her the first female secretary of state. This made her the highest-ranking woman in the US government. In her new position, Madeleine led the State Department and represented the United States when dealing with other countries. Madeleine proved she was a tough negotiator and a strong-willed problem solver as she tackled complicated issues.

While she was secretary of state, Madeline started to use the pins she wore on her jacket or blouse to make political statements. It all began when she was criticized by a foreign leader and referred to as a snake. From then on, she wore a snake pin whenever she had dealings with that leader. Over time, her pin collection grew to the point she had a pin for every occasion. When people were curious to know what her meetings were about, she would tell them to look at her pin.

Madeleine's service as secretary of state ended in 2001. Since then, she has continued her work in the field of international relations as an advisor, professor, and writer. A best-selling author, Madeleine has written five books. In *Madame Secretary*, she describes her time as secretary of state from an insider's point of view.

Throughout her life, Madeleine Albright has done far more than what was expected of her. As an immigrant and a woman, she used a combination of hard work, dedication, and courage to break down barriers. She was a pioneer in the field of politics, traditionally dominated by men. With her many achievements, Madeleine has set a new standard of achievement for future generations.

EXPLORE MORE! Learn more about Madeleine Albright's famous pins in her book *Read My Pins: Stories from a Diplomat's Jewel Box*. Discover how she started using pins as a form of expression and see pictures of some of her boldest choices.

TIPS FOR YOU! Did you know you can visit the United Nations on your phone? Download the free United Nations Visitor Centre app and explore everything the New York City landmark has to offer, including art exhibits, flags, sculptures, and more!

Isabel
ALLENDE
1942–

I sabel Allende is a Chilean-American writer and activist. Millions of her books have been sold around the world. Her novels entertain and educate readers by combining imaginative stories with fascinating historical events. In addition to being a successful novelist, she works to promote and protect the rights of women.

Isabel Allende was born in Lima, Peru, in 1942. Her parents, Tomás Allende and Francisca Llona Barros, were citizens of Chile who were living in Peru for a short time due to Tomás's work as a diplomat (a person who negotiates with other countries). When Isabel was only three years old, her father left the family and never returned. Unable to survive in Peru on her own, Isabel's mother decided to pack up her three children and return to Chile.

Much of Isabel's childhood was spent in the capital city of Santiago, Chile, where she lived with her mother, brothers, and grandfather. Isabel's mother often struggled to make ends meet and depended on Isabel's grandfather to help her get by. Seeing her mother struggle so much ignited Isabel's independent spirit, a quality she would hold for the rest of her life.

In 1953, Isabel's mother got married again. Like Isabel's father, her mother's new husband was a Chilean diplomat. It wasn't long before her stepfather's career required the family to move to Bolivia and then Lebanon. This marked the beginning of many international moves that Isabel would be forced to make.

When violence broke out in Lebanon in 1958, Isabel was sent back to Chile to finish high school. She struggled to understand chemistry, so she found a young engineering student who agreed to be her tutor. Isabel didn't know it at the time, but her chemistry tutor, Miguel Frías, would one day be her husband.

After graduating from high school, Isabel found work as a secretary at the UN office in Santiago. Two years later, she married Miguel and they started a family. Isabel's daughter, Paula, was born in 1963 and her son, Nicolás, was born in 1966.

Not long after the birth of her son, Isabel co-founded the first magazine in Chile that focused on the issues and lives of women. She also hosted a popular television show and published two children's books. Remembering the days of her childhood, Isabel worked extremely hard to avoid the struggles faced by her mother.

After starting a family and building a successful career, Isabel found herself on the move once again.

"WE ONLY HAVE WHAT WE GIVE."

Her father's cousin, Salvador Allende, was the Chilean president when the government was overthrown in 1973. Because Isabel was related to Salvador, the new government saw her as a threat. It was no longer safe for her to stay in Chile, so she moved with her husband and children to Venezuela, where she found work writing for a newspaper in the city of Caracas.

While living in Venezuela, Isabel learned that her grandfather was dying. Unable to return to Chile to visit him, she decided to write him a heartfelt letter. The emotional farewell to her dying grandfather eventually developed into her first novel. Published in 1982, *The House of the Spirits* was an international bestseller. Since that book, Isabel has begun writing all of her books on January 8, the date she started the letter to her grandfather.

Isabel proved to be a masterful storyteller and wrote two more novels in the years that followed. By weaving themes of love, justice, and equality, Isabel's stories connected with readers all over the world. Though she became tremendously successful as a writer, her relationship with her husband fell apart. In 1987, after 25 years of marriage, Isabel and Miguel decided to divorce.

During a visit to California on a book tour, Isabel met Willie Gordon, a lawyer and novelist. The two got married in 1988 and settled down just outside of San Francisco. Two years later, in 1990, democracy was reinstated in Chile. After being away for more than 15 years, Isabel could now safely visit the land of her childhood.

Tragedy cast a shadow over the next several years of Isabel's life. Her daughter, Paula, passed away from a rare blood disorder at the young age of 28. Isabel compared the grief she felt over losing her daughter to the feeling of walking alone in a long dark tunnel. She took all of her sadness and poured it into writing a new book, dedicated to Paula.

The loss of her daughter also motivated Isabel to start an organization that would promote the rights of women. In 1996, the Isabel Allende Foundation was established. Funded by the profits from the sale of her books, the foundation is dedicated to helping women around the world discover and claim power for themselves.

After setting up the foundation, Isabel published several more novels. By the year 2000, Isabel had written and published more than 10 successful books. Her stories, like her own life, feature strong female characters who take risks, but most importantly, follow their hearts. She uses her own personal experiences with loss, abandonment, and feeling alone to shape her stories and establish a deep connection with readers.

At the urging of her grandchildren, Isabel began writing a series of books for young adults. In 2003, *City of the Beasts* was published. It was the first book in a three-part series written for teenagers. Later that same year, Isabel became an American citizen.

Because of her commitment to fighting for the rights of women, Isabel was asked to represent Latin America as a flag bearer at the opening ceremonies of the 2006 Winter Olympic Games in Turin, Italy. Her time in the spotlight with other well-known and powerful women was very meaningful for Isabel. Even though she had written almost 20 celebrated books, she believed her most important work was the time and effort she put into supporting women around the world.

In her 2007 TED Talk, Isabel encouraged her audience to live passionately. Her open and honest talk featured stories of courageous women who risked their lives to help others. Using her influence as a writer, Isabel has never missed an opportunity to fight for the political, economic, and social equality of women.

Over the years, Isabel has received many awards for her exceptional career and her commitment to humanitarian causes. She received Chile's top prize for literature in 2010 and was awarded the Presidential Medal of Freedom by President Obama in 2014.

In her acceptance speech for the National Book Award in 2018, Isabel outlined her reasons and purpose for writing. First, she accepted the award on behalf of the millions of people who have come to

America in search of a better life. Isabel then explained that her writing reflected her own personal experiences and her strong desire to belong. She said that she put her memories of always feeling like a stranger in a new land into stories that readers could identify with. Finally, she expressed the pride she felt in being an American and her gratitude for the opportunity to give something back to the country that has been her home for the last 30 years.

Isabel Allende has tried to make a difference throughout her life. As a novelist, she entertains and educates readers all over the world. As an activist, she fights to advance women's rights. In both roles, she is dedicated and passionate about the work she does to serve others.

EXPLORE MORE! Do you want to explore the hidden worlds of the South American rain forest, climb the frosty peaks of the Himalayan mountains, or travel to the plains of Africa? You can! Isabel Go on the adventure of a lifetime with Isabel Allende's three-book series for young adults. Start reading the first book, *City of Beasts*, today!

TIPS FOR YOU! Are you interested in giving back to your community? You don't have to go far to find opportunities to help others. Pick up litter in your neighborhood, donate books to your local library, or offer to help your teacher at school. Even the smallest tasks can make a big difference!

Carlos
SANTANA
1947–

Carlos Santana is an award-winning Mexican-American musician. Considered one of the greatest guitarists of all time, he crosses boundaries and connects cultures with his creative mix of musical genres.

Carlos Santana was born in the Mexican state of Jalisco in 1947. He was one of six children born to his parents José Santana and Josefina Barragán. José Santana worked as a professional mariachi violinist and Josefina stayed home to take care of the large family.

The first instrument Carlos learned to play was the violin. It wasn't his ideal choice, but he continued to play it until his father surprised him with an electric guitar and an amplifier. Carlos was hooked. He fell in love with the sound, and his passion for music was born.

When Carlos was eight years old, his family moved to Tijuana, a city in northern Mexico near the border of California. Carlos was inspired by the music he heard on the radio. As a young teenager, he started performing in local clubs and captivated audiences with his smooth blend of rock and blues music.

José Santana moved to San Francisco for work, and the rest of the family joined him there in 1961. Although only 14 years old, Carlos was fascinated with the thriving art scene he found in San Francisco. The city was filled with people yearning to explore their creativity.

Carlos continued to play guitar throughout middle school and high school. Recognizing his commitment and talent, one of Carlos's art teachers took him aside and explained the importance of working hard to achieve a dream. From that moment on, Carlos committed himself to a life of music.

While living in San Francisco, Carlos was able to see live performances by musicians he idolized, including blues legends like B. B. King and Ray Charles. Carlos was also introduced to a variety of musical genres, like jazz and folk, which he weaved into his own music in later years.

After graduating from high school in 1965, Carlos made two big changes in his life. He became a US citizen, and he committed to making music his full-time job.

In 1966, Carlos formed the Santana Blues Band with two other musicians. The trio got attention by playing original music that included a blend of rock, jazz, blues, and salsa. The band quickly became known simply as Santana, and they gained a huge following in San Francisco.

Just three years after forming the band, Carlos became a global sensation after he performed at the Woodstock Music and Art Festival in New York. Woodstock provided an audience of more than 400,000 people, and it was an important moment for Carlos's music career. His success in San Francisco combined with his terrific performance at Woodstock led to a recording contract with Columbia Records.

Working with legendary music producer Clive Davis, Carlos released his debut studio album, *Santana*, in 1969. The album was an instant success and went triple platinum, selling more than four million copies. The album included a top-ten single and stayed at the top of the Billboard charts for more than two years.

The release of Carlos's first album marked the beginning of his successful career in music. Carlos had an incredible ability to bring together the tones, beats, and rhythms of different musical genres and blend them with rock music. By combining different sounds and styles, his albums took listeners on a cultural adventure.

In 1973, Carlos met and married his wife, Deborah. They have three children, Salvador, Stella, and Angelica. With the help of his wife, Carlos managed to balance his family life and his music career. He toured the country doing live performances, continued to release albums, and worked on projects with other musicians. He never slowed down.

With a family and thriving music career, Carlos wanted to start giving back. He participated in several benefit concerts, including a performance at Live Aid, a fundraising concert to help fight hunger in Africa. Held in 1985, the concert was shown on TV and watched by people around the world. Besides Carlos, some of the biggest names in music performed at Live Aid, including U2 and Queen.

Carlos returned to New York in 1994 to perform at the Woodstock 25th anniversary concert. Later that year, he released *Santana Brothers,* an album he recorded with his brother and his nephew. Like many of his other albums, it climbed the Billboard charts and was nominated for a Grammy Award.

Carlos signed with Arista Records in 1997. Working with his mentor Clive Davis again, Carlos released his 18th album, *Supernatural.* To appeal to a larger audience, he teamed up with several top musicians on some of the songs. *Supernatural* sold more than 10 million copies in its first year of release and is widely considered to be Carlos's greatest work.

For his work on *Supernatural,* Carlos received eight Grammy Award nominations, including nominations for Best Album of the Year and Best Record of the Year. Amazingly, Carlos won in every category and tied Michael Jackson for the most Grammys won in a single year.

In 1998, Carlos started the Milagro Foundation with his family. *Milagro* means "miracle" in Spanish, and the

> **"IF YOU CARRY JOY IN YOUR HEART, YOU CAN HEAL ANY MOMENT."**

Milagro Foundation focuses on helping young people all over the world. By donating millions of dollars to nonprofit programs, the foundation supports education and health services for children in need.

That same year, Carlos was voted into the Rock and Roll Hall of Fame, where he joined a long list of talented musicians. In 2013, Carlos earned the Kennedy Center Honor award for his contributions to the music world. This award is given every year to people in the performing arts for their lifetime of contributions to American culture.

Carlos published his first book, *The Universal Tone: Bringing My Story to Light*, in 2014. The book describes Carlos's journey from the clubs in Mexico to concert halls and arenas all over the world. Carlos filled the pages with personal stories and life lessons, giving readers a glimpse into the life of a legendary musician.

Carlos's career has lasted more than 40 years. He has sold more than 100 million records and won a total of ten Grammy Awards. *Rolling Stone* magazine named him one of the greatest guitarists of all time and described him as a "rare instrumentalist who can be identified in just one note." In addition to his tremendous achievements as a musician, Carlos continues to be devoted to a wide range of causes and supports a number of charities.

Carlos Santana has shaped the world of music by blending styles and experimenting with different genres. His inventive work withstands the test of time, pushes creative limits, and connects distant cultures.

EXPLORE MORE! The Rock and Roll Hall of Fame recognizes musical excellence. Learn more about the musicians, producers, and engineers who have been voted into the Hall of Fame at www.RockHall.com.

TIPS FOR YOU! Listen to some of Carlos Santana's music. Can you hear the different musical genres in his songs? Which ones can you identify?

Mikhail
BARYSHNIKOV
1948–

Mikhail Baryshnikov is a Latvian-American dancer, choreographer, and actor. He is often considered one of the greatest dancers in the world. Using his excellent technical skills, he seems to move his powerful body without any physical effort.

Mikhail Baryshnikov was born in 1948 in the capital city of Riga, Latvia. At the time, Latvia wasn't an independent country like it is today. It was a state controlled by the Soviet Union, a Communist nation that existed from 1922 until 1991. The Soviet Union was made up of Russia and 14 smaller states.

Mikhail's father, Nikolay, was a colonel in the Soviet military. He had a stern manner and was a strict parent, which made it difficult for him to have a close relationship with his young son. Mikhail's mother was a dressmaker. She loved the arts, and introduced Mikhail to the theatre, opera, and ballet. Sadly, Mikhail was only 12 years old when she passed away.

Even though his father wanted him to attend military school, Mikhail followed his passion and dove into the world of ballet. For young Mikhail, practicing the art of dance was how he made sense of the world. Immersing himself in ballet at such a young age inspired him to be a better person and gave him a sense of direction.

Mikhail wanted to improve his abilities and learn more about the beautiful art form he loved. So, at the age of 15, he moved away from home to attend a respected ballet school. The Vaganova Academy of Russian Ballet was located in the city of Leningrad (which is now St. Petersburg, Russia). While studying at the academy, Mikhail was coached by the legendary ballet dancer and master teacher Aleksander Pushkin.

Mikhail has described Pushkin as being like a father to him, a man who taught him many valuable lessons. Besides learning the technical skills of ballet, Mikhail began to understand the demanding physical requirements of being a top dancer. Once he learned to deal with the mental challenges that came with hard work, everything else was easy.

In 1967, Mikhail earned a spot in the famous Kirov Ballet Company, one of the two major ballet companies in the Soviet Union at the time. Practicing at least four or five hours a day, Mikhail was an extremely dedicated dancer. Due to his immense talent, he was cast in lead roles, and parts were specifically designed for him to perform. Mikhail was known for his intense stage

> **"I'VE BEEN HURT QUITE A FEW TIMES. THE MORE INJURIES YOU GET, THE SMARTER YOU GET."**

presence, beautiful technique, and physical strength. He quickly rose through the ranks to become the company's principal dancer, an amazing achievement for any performer.

Mikhail dazzled audiences with his graceful abilities and dramatic dancing, and soon became one of the Soviet Union's leading ballet dancers. In 1969, at the age of 21, he was awarded the gold medal at Moscow's first International Ballet Competition.

Although he had a successful career in ballet, Mikhail felt life in the Soviet Union was too rigid and strict. He earned a good salary, lived in a nice apartment, and danced for one of the top ballet companies in the world. But Mikhail didn't have what he wanted most—freedom.

With the help of a young Canadian lawyer, Mikhail started to secretly plan his escape from the Soviet Union. After a performance in Toronto, Canada, in 1974, Mikhail slipped out into the night and away from the watchful eyes of his Soviet security team. He abandoned everything he had ever known. Now protected by the Canadian government, Mikhail began to look forward to a new life filled with personal and artistic freedom.

After spending several months in Canada, Mikhail settled in New York City, where he joined the American Ballet Theatre. Dancing for one of the best ballet companies in the world gave Mikhail a chance to spend time perfecting his craft and expressing himself creatively. Mikhail captivated American audiences with his stunning performances in *The Nutcracker*, *Cinderella*, and *Don Quixote*. His talent on stage went beyond national boundaries.

In 1978, Mikhail stunned the dance world when he made the decision to leave the American Ballet Theatre and join the New York City Ballet. Mikhail wanted a chance to learn the dance style of the New York City Ballet's founder, George Balanchine. Working with Balanchine, Mikhail performed the lead role in many major dance productions. His work on stage was so exceptional that he captured the attention of United States President Jimmy Carter.

President Carter was hosting a series of Sunday afternoon concerts at the White House and he wanted to add a ballet performance by Mikhail to the list. Even though the small stage at the White House made it impossible for Mikhail to perform his gravity-defying leaps, his performance was met with a standing ovation. President Carter later described Mikhail as someone with great courage who was never afraid to dive into new experiences.

After his performance at the White House, it was clear that Mikhail was one of the best and most famous dancers in the world. He had been performing for nearly 20 years, and he now wanted to support other artists. In 1979, Mikhail started the Baryshnikov Dance Foundation. Its mission was to encourage and promote performers, choreographers, directors, writers, composers, and designers. Mikhail wanted to give artists the time, space, and resources they needed to research and develop their own projects.

In 1980, Mikhail returned to the American Ballet Theatre as a principal dancer and artistic director. As the artistic director, Mikhail had many responsibilities and a busy schedule. He had to find a theatre for performances, oversee rehearsals, manage the dancers, and handle business matters. During this time, he was suffering from several leg injuries, which made it difficult for him to perform as a dancer. Mikhail wanted to pursue other professional opportunities, so he made the decision to leave the American Ballet Theatre in 1990.

He spent the next several years exploring other forms of artistic expression and changing the way people thought about dance. He performed in Broadway plays, Hollywood movies, and Emmy-winning television shows. His incredible talent earned him many honors, including an Oscar nomination.

After a brief relationship with actress Jessica Lange in 1981, his first daughter, Alexandra, was born. She was named after Mikhail's mother. In 1986, more than

10 years after leaving the Soviet Union, Mikhail became a US citizen.

Mikhail wanted to step away from classical ballet and experiment with modern dance. In 1990, he co-founded the White Oak Dance Project. This one-of-a-kind dance company focused on giving choreographers room to create new projects that they could present to audiences across the country. The company did tours until 2002, showing the many different ways modern dance could be performed.

In 2000, Mikhail was presented with the Kennedy Center Honor award for a lifetime of extraordinary achievement in performing arts.

Five years later, Mikhail opened the Baryshnikov Arts Center in New York City. The center is a place where artists from around the world can meet, create, and perform. Mikhail sees the Baryshnikov Arts Center as his small contribution to society, something for the city he admires and the country he loves.

In 2006, Mikhail married his longtime partner, Lisa Rinehart, who was also an American Ballet Theatre dancer. They have three children. Although he has knee problems, Mikhail remains active and continues to perform. He is passionate about supporting other artists and is always searching for new and exciting developments in the art world.

Mikhail used his incredible strength and masterful technical skills to amaze audiences for more than 40 years. Never afraid to dive into new experiences, he explored artistic expression and pushed it in new directions. He also helped change how modern dancers were seen by audiences. Mikhail Baryshnikov's incredible career achievements are an inspiration to other artists who feel passionately about their work.

EXPLORE MORE! Meet Misty Copeland! She made history as the first African American to become the principal dancer at the American Ballet Theatre. Read her best-selling book *Life in Motion: An Unlikely Ballerina* or watch her documentary, *A Ballerina's Tale*, to learn more about her inspiring story.

TIPS FOR YOU! Do you know the first five ballet positions? Learn all five and more at www.HowCast.com.

Iman
ABDULMAJID
1955–

Iman Abdulmajid is a Somali-American supermodel, businesswoman, and activist. Often considered a pioneer in the field of modeling, Iman expanded the definition of beauty and helped open up the fashion industry to people of color.

Iman was born in Mogadishu, Somalia, in 1955. Her parents, Marian and Mohamed Abdulmajid, were loving and supportive modern thinkers. Marian worked in a hospital as a doctor, and Mohamed worked as a diplomat, representing Somalia in other Middle Eastern countries. Marian and Mohamed made it clear to Iman, her two sisters, and her two brothers that education was important and with it great things could be achieved.

When Iman was still a young girl, her father's work as a diplomat took the family to Egypt. Wanting the best education for their daughter, Iman's parents sent her to a private boarding school. Iman was an excellent student and learned to speak four languages: Arabic, Italian, French, and English.

In 1969, when Iman was 14, her schooling in Egypt was cut short. The Somali government had been overthrown and her father was asked to return to Somalia. The entire country was facing restrictions and the foreign embassies were closed. Uncertain of the new government and afraid for their safety, Iman's family left everything behind and fled to Kenya in the middle of the night.

Iman's life changed in an instant. She went from having a comfortable life as the daughter of an important diplomat to worrying about her future as a refugee (a person who is forced to leave their country). As a refugee in Kenya, Iman had left behind everything familiar, including family members, friends, and her Somali culture.

At the age of 18, after finishing high school, Iman continued her education in Kenya at Nairobi University. To pay for tuition, Iman used her ability to speak several languages to get a part-time position as a translator.

While walking to class one day, Iman was stopped in the street by an American fashion photographer. He was interested in taking photos of her and offered her $8,000, the cost of one year's tuition at Nairobi University. Iman agreed to let him photograph her. His photos of her were eventually seen by executives at Wilhelmina, a top modeling agency in New York City.

Impressed with the photos, the Wilhelmina agency invited Iman to New York. By the third day of her visit,

"IF BEAUTY IS IN THE EYE OF THE BEHOLDER, LET THE BEHOLDER BE YOU."

Iman was in a photo shoot for *Vogue* magazine, something most models could only dream of. Iman had never worn heels, put on makeup, or flipped through a fashion magazine, so her sudden success was shocking. Everything about living and working in the United States was new to her, and there were times when she felt extremely uncomfortable.

On one of her first photo shoots, Iman was surprised to learn that the makeup artist didn't have cosmetics that would match her skin tone. Until this point in her life, Iman had never been judged or treated differently based on the color of her skin. Iman understood the importance of a great image, so she made finding makeup that would work well for her a top priority. She was determined to have the same opportunities as other top models.

Iman was unwilling to be defined by her skin color and refused modeling jobs that paid less because she was dark-skinned. She also spoke out about top fashion brands that did not use models of all skin tones in their advertising campaigns or runway shows. Iman was passionate about changing the definition of beauty.

Iman appeared on countless magazine covers and walked the runways for the world's most famous designers. For 14 years she was one of the most in-demand models in the United States. Iman worked for all the top designers, including Yves Saint Laurent, Versace, Calvin Klein, and Donna Karan.

In 1978 Iman married basketball star Spencer Haywood and they had a daughter, Zulekha. A year later, Iman became an American citizen. Thankful for the country that gave her everything, she said, "As much as I am Somali, I am American."

Iman's life took a big turn in 1983 when she was involved in a car accident that fractured her cheek-bone, eye socket, collarbone, and several ribs. It took five months for her to recover from her injuries. Iman used this time to think about her life and her priorities. Not long after the accident, she made several life-changing decisions. In 1987, she ended her marriage to Spencer Haywood. Two years later, she shocked the fashion world when she retired from modeling. It was time for something new.

Soon after making the decision to end her modeling career, Iman met rock music legend David Bowie. The couple fell in love and got married in 1992. Iman now had a new life and new priorities. Just a few weeks after her honeymoon, she was focused on raising awareness of the desperate situation people were facing in her native country of Somalia.

Iman convinced the British Broadcasting Company (BBC) to let her take a documentary film crew to Somalia, which had been nearly destroyed by war, drought, and famine. When she flew back to Somalia to start filming, Iman barely recognized the country of her childhood. The streets of Mogadishu were filled with extremely thin people dressed in rags, and teenagers walked around carrying automatic weapons. Using her influence as a famous supermodel, Iman was able to shine a light on Somalia's desperate need for help.

Although she retired from modeling in 1989, Iman continued to make an impact in the world of fashion and beauty. She remembered her early experiences in the industry and was still frustrated with the lack of makeup options for women of color. To deal with this problem, Iman launched her own line of cosmetics in 1994.

Iman Cosmetics is a makeup and skincare collection designed to meet the needs of all women. When the cosmetics were introduced, they were like nothing else available, and they had an enormous impact on the beauty industry. After years of providing makeup to people of all skin tones, Iman Cosmetics joined forces with one of the largest beauty companies and became a worldwide brand.

In 2000, Iman released her first book, *I am Iman*, her autobiography. The book questioned the business of fashion and beauty and how it affects people's identities. Iman told her story in an unusual way, using a combination of words, photographs, and sketches.

Later that year, Iman's second daughter, Alexandria, was born. After the birth of her daughter, Iman stepped out of the spotlight. She wanted to focus on being a mother and give more of her time and attention to charities and other causes.

Iman published her second book, *Beauty of Color*, in 2005. It was the first book to discuss beauty concerns for all types of skin tones. In addition to providing makeup techniques and skin care tips, the book encourages women to be proud of their appearance and their unique beauty.

Throughout her career as a model and businesswoman, Iman worked closely with several organizations as an advocate for parents and children in Africa. In 2006, she was a spokesperson and global ambassador for Keep a Child Alive, an organization aimed at preventing the disease, AIDS. She also devoted her time to supporting the Children's Defense Fund, All Kids Foundation, Action Against Hunger, and many other charities.

The challenging experiences Iman faced as a child shaped her into a woman who refused to see her differences as limiting her opportunities. She used her strong will and position as a supermodel to promote and celebrate diversity. With a fierce determination to succeed, Iman helped revolutionize the fashion industry and redefine standards of beauty.

EXPLORE MORE! The International Olympic Committee created a team of refugee athletes in 2016. Discover more about the Refugee Olympic Team at www.Olympic.org.

TIPS FOR YOU! Celebrate diversity! Write a poem that explores the world's beautiful differences.

Nadia
COMĂNECI

1961–

Nadia Comăneci is a Romanian-American gymnast and coach. She is the first person in the history of gymnastics to score a perfect 10 at an Olympic gymnastics event.

Nadia Comăneci was born in a small town in the mountains of Romania in 1961. Her father was an auto mechanic, and her mother stayed home to run the household. As a young child, Nadia was filled with energy and had a hard time sitting still.

At the age of six, while practicing cartwheels on the playground at school, Nadia was spotted by gymnastics coach Béla Károlyi. Béla immediately recognized Nadia's athletic talent and invited her to start training at his gymnastics school. Soon, Nadia was training three hours a day with Béla and his wife, Márta Károlyi.

Nadia impressed her coaches with her hard work and determination. She competed in her first official gymnastics competition when she was seven, placing 13th at the Romanian National Junior Championships.

Determined to improve, she trained even harder and the following year she placed first.

Nadia experienced international success at age 13. She placed first in almost every event at the European Gymnastics Championships in Norway. A year later, Nadia competed in the American Cup, America's largest and most respected international gymnastics tournament. She took home first place.

After the tournament, she took press pictures with men's winner Bart Conner. Teasing the young winners, the photographer told Bart to kiss Nadia on the cheek. He did, and the kiss was captured on film. The young gymnasts would meet again years later.

Nadia stepped onto the world stage in 1976 at the Olympic Games in Montreal, Canada. Only 14 years old and representing the country of Romania, she made gymnastics history. Nadia competed in a variety of events, but it was her performance on the uneven bars that captivated the world. After finishing her routine, she became the first gymnast in history to receive a 10, a perfect score. Nadia didn't seem to realize how incredible her accomplishment was and went on to earn six more perfect 10s. She finished the Olympic Games that year with five medals. Three of them were gold.

Nadia's tremendous achievements at the Olympic Games made her an international star. When she landed in Romania after making history in Montreal, 10,000 fans were waiting for her at the airport. Nadia

> **"BE A PICKPOCKET OF IDEAS.
> LISTEN TO EVERYONE,
> KEEP AN OPEN MIND, AND
> TAKE THE BEST OF WHAT
> EVERYONE HAS TO OFFER."**

was named Athlete of the Year by the Associated Press, and she appeared on the cover of many magazines, including *Sports Illustrated*, *Time*, and *Newsweek*.

In addition to the awards and publicity, Nadia had a piece of music named in her honor. The music played over slow motion scenes of Nadia's gymnastic routines, shown on a major television network. The song became extremely popular and people started connecting it to Nadia. Originally titled "Cotton's Dream," the title was changed to "Nadia's Theme" in 1976.

Nadia was the definition of a true champion, some-one who performs the best routine at the right time. She was hoping to do that again at the 1980 Olympic Games in Moscow. Now 18 years old, Nadia understood the importance of competing at the Olympics. She also felt the pressure.

Nadia shocked the crowd when she fell during her best event, the uneven bars. She knew she was doing her routine too quickly. She took a breath, slowed down, and finished the Olympics with four medals, two gold and two silver. Happy with her accomplishments in Moscow, Nadia later called her fall a learning experience.

A year after the Moscow Olympics, Nadia traveled across the United States on a gymnastics tour with her coaches, Béla and Márta Károlyi. Called "Nadia '81," the tour stopped in 11 cities, where Nadia and other top gymnasts performed and met with fans.

At the end of the tour, Béla and Márta decided to stay in the United States. They didn't want to live under the strict control of the Communist government in Romania anymore. The Romanian government became afraid that Nadia would also want to escape the country, so they put strict limits on her travel. She wasn't allowed to attend any international competitions or leave Romania without permission.

Nadia had earned a total of nine Olympic medals, and she now lived a luxurious life with nice cars and expensive jewelry. But she didn't have the freedom she wanted. Romania was a Communist country ruled by a dictator. Living there was difficult. Nadia was constantly watched, and had little access to information from the world outside of Romania.

Tired of living her life "under a microscope," Nadia made the decision to leave Romania in 1989. Risking everything for freedom, Nadia braved the cold temperatures and walked over the Romanian border into Hungary. From there, she traveled by car to Austria. At the US Embassy in Vienna, she asked for protection, and within a few hours she was on a plane to New York City. It took great courage for Nadia to leave her entire life behind and start over in a new country.

Shortly after she arrived in America, Nadia was reconnected with Bart Conner, the gymnast who had kissed her after a competition many years ago. As an Olympic gold medalist and American Cup winner, Bart was still very involved with gymnastics. Nadia and Bart started performing at exhibitions together and their relationship grew closer. They got married in 1996.

The wedding ceremony took place in Bucharest, Romania, where Nadia was treated like royalty. The Communist government fell shortly after Nadia left Romania. Since then, she has reunited with her family and is able to travel freely to and from Romania. After getting married, Nadia and Bart settled in Norman, Oklahoma, where they run a gymnastics academy for children of all ages.

In 2001, Nadia completed the final step of the citizenship process when she took the Oath of Allegiance in an Oklahoma City courthouse, making her a US citizen. Five years later, her son Dylan was born.

Nadia and Bart travel the world together promoting the sport of gymnastics. They give talks about achieving goals and make personal appearances at events. They also own a company that produces and promotes gymnastics events for television.

Nadia's work isn't focused only on gymnastics. She opened a clinic in Romania for adults and children who can't afford to pay for treatment or find care somewhere else. She also serves on the board of directors for the Special Olympics and works closely with several charities, including the Muscular Dystrophy Association and Laureus Sport for Good Foundation. Nadia appreciates all of the amazing opportunities she's had in her life and sees her volunteer work as a way to give back to the countries that gave her so much.

Nadia is often considered one of the greatest athletes in the history of gymnastics. She was the first person in Olympic history to score a perfect 10, something that many people thought was impossible. She left a legacy that will last lifetimes.

EXPLORE MORE! Watch how Nadia made history with her perfect 10 performance on the uneven bars at the 1976 Olympic Games in Montreal, Canada. Go to www.Olympic.org.

TIPS FOR YOU! Did you know that trampoline and speed walking are Olympic events? Check out all the different types of Olympic sports at www.Olympic.org.

Dikembe
MUTOMBO

1966–

Dikembe Mutombo is a Congolese-American basketball player and humanitarian.

He is often considered one of the greatest defenders in the National Basketball Association (NBA), and he is committed to making the world a better place.

Dikembe Mutombo was born in 1966 in Kinshasa, the capital city of the Democratic Republic of the Congo (formerly called Zaire), a country in central Africa. His full name is Dikembe Mutombo Mpolondo Mukamba Jean-Jacques Wamutombo.

Dikembe was the seventh of 10 children born to his parents Samuel and Biamba Marie Mutombo. His mother stayed home and his father supported the family as a teacher. Dikembe's parents stressed the importance of faith, education, hard work, and community to their children, and always made family a top priority.

During Dikembe's childhood, the Congo was going through serious political changes. Dikembe grew up witnessing poverty, illness, and death on a daily basis. At a young age, he knew he wanted to make a difference and change the living conditions for the people of Africa. His dream was to go to medical school in America, return to the Congo, and help save lives.

Growing up, Dikembe lived in a large home with his parents, siblings, and other family members. He was raised in a strict environment. At a young age, he was introduced to Christianity. Both of his parents were very involved in their church, and the Mutombo family never missed a Sunday service.

Life as a young boy wasn't easy for Dikembe. He was taller than the other children, and he was teased for his unusual height. After his classmates called him a giraffe, Dikembe started slouching in shame. With the support of his brothers, Dikembe was able to gain confidence as he got older and take pride in his size.

Despite being seven feet tall in high school, Dikembe wasn't interested in playing basketball. He was a star goalie on the soccer field, and he enjoyed martial arts. But Dikembe's father pushed him to join the basketball team during his last year of high school. During the first practice, while learning how to jump, Dikembe fell and split open his chin. It took 22 stitches to repair the damage.

Even though his first experience playing basketball left him bloody and bruised, Dikembe showed immense talent on the court. After high school, he joined the Zaire National Basketball Team, where

> ## "SOMETIMES IN LIFE, YOU HAVE TO BE DRIVEN AND PUSH YOURSELF TO EXCELLENCE."

he spent two years traveling and learning how to play the game. In 1987, Dikembe's dream of attending medical school in America came true. He was offered a scholarship from Georgetown University in Washington, DC.

Dikembe spent most of his first year at Georgetown learning English. His plan was to study medicine, become a doctor, and return to the Congo to make a difference and change lives. While walking through the halls on his way to class one day, Dikembe caught the eye of the university's legendary basketball coach John Thompson.

Not long after, Dikembe received a basketball scholarship and started making a name for himself as a top defensive player. As a student athlete, Dikembe was pushed both mentally and physically. Besides playing basketball and keeping up with his schoolwork, Dikembe served as a Congressional intern in Washington, DC.

By his senior year at Georgetown, Dikembe was getting noticed by NBA scouts. He set the Georgetown record for most blocked shots in a single game and averaged

15 points and 12 rebounds per game. In recognition, he was named Big East Defensive Player of the Year.

In 1991, Dikembe graduated from the University of Georgetown. His goal now was to play in the NBA, and he didn't have to wait long. He was picked fourth in the draft by the Denver Nuggets. For Dikembe, it was a dream come true.

Dikembe made an impact immediately during his first season in Denver. He was third in the league in rebounding and averaged 13 points per game, earning him a spot in the 1992 NBA All-Star Game. In his five seasons with the Nuggets, Dikembe used expert timing, sharp elbows, and perfect positioning to become one of the NBA's greatest defenders. In 1995, Dikembe earned his first NBA Defensive Player of the Year award.

During his time in Denver, Dikembe began to wag his finger at other players, a gesture he would become famous for. After blocking a shot, he jokingly waved his finger back and forth at his opponents, like a parent scolding a child. Dikembe considered himself to be a great defender, and he wanted to let players on the opposing teams know that "man does not fly in the house of Mutombo." NBA officials decided the finger wag was an unsportsmanlike gesture and banned it in 1998.

When his contract with the Denver Nuggets ended in 1996, Dikembe signed a five-year contract with the Atlanta Hawks. During his time in Atlanta, Dikembe continued to be a ferocious shot blocker and rebounder.

He earned two more NBA Defensive Player of the Year awards and appeared at the All-Star Game two more times.

Dikembe was committed to making a difference on and off the court. He donated his time and money to several different charities, including Basketball Without Borders, Read to Achieve, and the Special Olympics. In 1996, he paid for the entire Zaire Women's Basketball Team to travel to Atlanta so they could participate in the Summer Olympic Games.

In 1997, Dikembe set up the Dikembe Mutombo Foundation. Its main goal is to improve the quality of health and education in the Democratic Republic of the Congo. Although Dikembe's boyhood dream of becoming a doctor was over, he stayed committed to helping the people of the Congo, and he began working on plans to build a $29 million hospital in his hometown of Kinshasa.

With plans for the hospital in progress, Dikembe focused his attention on his basketball career. Near the end of the 2000–2001 season, Dikembe was traded to the Philadelphia 76ers. He continued to be a strong defensive player and helped lead the team to the NBA Finals. In 2001, he became the first player in NBA history to be awarded Defensive Player of the Year four times.

Dikembe was traded to the New Jersey Nets in 2001, but he missed most of the season because of a wrist injury. In 2003, while he was playing for the New York Knicks, Dikembe's finger wag came back, but he was only allowed to use it with the crowd. In 2004, Dikembe joined the Houston Rockets, where he spent the next five seasons.

In 2006, Dikembe became a US citizen. The following year, he was invited to attend the President's State of the Union Address, where President George W. Bush mentioned Dikembe's recent US citizenship and his admirable work in Africa.

The Biamba Marie Mutombo Hospital opened in 2007. It was the first modern medical facility to open in Kinshasa in 40 years. Dikembe had personally given half of the money needed to complete the project, and he named it after his mother. She had taught him the importance of helping others and inspired him to look at the world with love and kindness.

Dikembe retired from the NBA in 2009. His basketball career lasted 18 seasons and included eight All-Star Games and four NBA Defensive Player of the Year awards. Known by his nickname, Mount Mutombo, Dikembe used his power and height to become one of the best defenders to ever play the game.

Dikembe was voted into the NBA Hall of Fame in 2015. His remarkable achievements on the basketball court combined with his generosity and compassion for others make him an ideal role model for athletes around the world. Through his foundation and his work for other causes, Dikembe continues to use his success as a professional basketball player to help transform the lives of people in need.

EXPLORE MORE! Did you know basketball was originally played using peach baskets and a soccer ball? Learn more about the history of basketball online at www.Olympic.org.

TIPS FOR YOU! Discover the Naismith Memorial Basketball Hall of Fame online. Read about the accomplishments of more than 400 Hall of Fame members at www.HoopHall.com.

More Inspiring People to Explore

Joseph Pulitzer
Hungarian-American Newspaper Editor and Publisher
1847–1911
Joseph Pulitzer, creator of the Pulitzer Prize, was known for pushing the boundaries of American investigative journalism.

Chien-Shiung Wu
Chinese-American Physicist
1912–1997
Chien-Shiung Wu was an award-winning nuclear physicist who was known for her contributions to the development of the atomic bomb.

Celia Cruz
Cuban-American Singer
1925–2003
Celia Cruz, known as the "Queen of Salsa," captivated audiences for more than 40 years with her fast-paced rhythmic music.

Jaime Escalante
Bolivian-American Educator
1930–2010
Jaime Escalante received national attention for his dedicated efforts to educate struggling students in a poor area of Los Angeles.

Oscar de la Renta
Dominican-American Fashion Designer
1932–2014
Oscar de la Renta was a celebrated fashion designer whose clothing continues to be worn by influential women all over the world.

Zubin Mehta
Indian-American Conductor and Musician
1936–
Zubin Mehta is a world-renowned orchestra conductor, music director, and musician.

Arianna Huffington
Greek-American Author and Businesswoman
1950–
Arianna Huffington co-founded the media company *The Huffington Post*, started the wellness site Thrive Global, and is the author of several best-selling books.

Jerry Yang
Taiwanese-American Electrical Engineer and Entrepreneur
1968–
Jerry Yang is the co-founder and former CEO of Yahoo!, a web services provider and one of the pioneers in the development of the Internet.

Freddy Adu
Ghanaian-American Professional Soccer Player
1989–
Freddy Adu became the youngest athlete ever to play major-league soccer when he signed with the D.C. United club at 14 years old.

Maame Biney
Ghanaian-American Olympic Speed Skater
2000–
Maame Biney made history as the first African-American woman to qualify for the US Olympic speed skating team.

References

A&E Television Networks. "Albert Einstein." History.com, October 27, 2009. https://www.history.com/topics /inventions/albert-einstein.

Allende, Isabel. "Isabel Allende—Biography." Accessed June 5, 2019. http://www.isabelallende.com/en/bio.

Allende, Isabel. "Tales of Passion." Filmed March 2007 in Monterey, CA. TED video, 17:53. https://www.ted .com/talks/isabel_allende_tells_tales_of_passion#t-789.

Bailey, Spencer, and Alex Scimecca. "The Masterful Modernism of I. M. Pei." *Fortune*, May 19, 2019. http:// fortune.com/2019/05/19/im-pei-architect-death/.

Barnard College. "New York City's Chinatown Post Office Named in Honor of Dr. Mabel Lee 1916." December 3, 2018. https://barnard.edu/news/new-york -citys-chinatown-post-office-named-honor-dr-mabel -lee-1916.

Berger, Joseph. "Elie Wiesel, Auschwitz Survivor and Nobel Peace Prize Winner, Dies at 87." *The New York Times*, July 2, 2016. https://www.nytimes.com/2016/07 /03/world/europe/elie-wiesel-auschwitz-survivor-and -nobel-peace-prize-winner-dies-at-87.html.

Davies, Michelle. "Life Stories: Iman." *Marie Claire*, November 15, 2016. https://www.marieclaire.co.uk /news/celebrity-news/life-stories-iman-437161.

Dawson, Rosario. "Supermodel Iman Wants Widespread Education and Earnest Activism." *Interview Magazine*, March 12, 2018. https://www.interview magazine.com/fashion/supermodel-iman-wants -widespread-education-earnest-activism.

de Bertodano, Helen. "The Incredible Life of Isabel Allende." *The Telegraph*, January 28, 2014. https://www .telegraph.co.uk/culture/books/authorinterviews /10589928/The-incredible-life-of-Isabel-Allende.html.

Dikembe Mutombo Foundation, Inc. "All About Dikembe." Accessed June 6, 2019. https://www.dmf.org/all-about -dikembe/.

Doneson, Judith. "Maya Deren." Jewish Women's Archive, February 27, 2009. https://www.jwa.org/encyclopedia /article/deren-maya.

Downey, Lynn. "Levi Strauss." *Immigrant Entrepreneurship: German-American Business Biographies, 1720 to the Present*, Vol. 2, German Historical Institute. Last modified February 18, 2014. http://www.immigrant entrepreneurship.org/entry.php?rec=19.

Duffy, Martha. "Thoroughly Modern Misha." *Time*, June 24, 2001. http://content.time.com/time/magazine /article/0,9171,163995,00.html.

Dunham, Katherine, and Alexander Hammid. *In the Mirror of Maya Deren*. Directed by Martina Kudlacek. Austria: Zeitgeist Films, 2002.

The Elie Wiesel Foundation for Humanity. "Elie Wiesel." Accessed June 5, 2019. http://eliewieselfoundation.org /elie-wiesel/.

Hawse, Mary Lou. "Mother Jones, the Miners' Angel." Illinois Labor History Society. Accessed June 7, 2019. http://www.illinoislaborhistory.org/labor-history -articles/mother-jones-the-miners-angel.

Hendrickson, Tamara L. "Madeleine Albright." The Women of Hopkins. Accessed May 29, 2019. https:// www.womenofhopkins.com/albright.

ICS Media Production. "Dikembe Mutombo Interview." YouTube video, 23:53. Posted November 5, 2013. https:// www.youtube.com/watch?v=HSPQzMStoPE&t=113s.

Jones, Mary Harris. *Autobiography of Mother Jones*. Chicago: Charles H. Kerr & Company, 1925.

Kennedy Center. "Mikhail Baryshnikov." Accessed June 6, 2019. http://www.kennedy-center.org/Artist/A3693.

King, Larry, and Carlos Santana. "Legendary Carlos Santana Discusses Famed Career, Ferguson, Obama and Immigration". YouTube video, 5:13. Posted December 8, 2014. https://www.youtube.com /watch?v=wNkDp79o5aA.

Kisselgoff, Anna. "Baryshnikov Cites Soviet Curb on Art." *The New York Times*, July 23, 1974.

Kisselgoff, Anna. "Dance: Baryshnikov at the White House." *The New York Times*, February 26, 1979.

Kumar, Isabelle, and Nadia Comăneci. "Nadia Comaneci: Gymnast of Perfection and Defector." Euronews, August 8, 2016. https://www.euronews.com/2016 /08/08/nadia-comaneci-gymnast-of-perfection -defectorand-mother-on-the-global-.

Levi Strauss & Co. "The Story of Levi Strauss." March 14, 2013. https://www.levistrauss.com/2013/03/14/the -story-of-levi-strauss/.

Levi Strauss Museum. "Levi and the Jeans." Accessed June 6, 2019. http://www.levi-strauss-museum.de/en /levi-und-die-jeans/.

May, Grace. "Leading Development at Home: Dr. Mabel Ping Hua Lee (1896–1966)." *William Carey International Development Journal*, November 1, 2016. https://wciujournal.wciu.edu/ women-in-international-development/2018/10/14/ leading-development-at-home-dr-mabel-ping-hua- lee-18961966.

Michals, Debra. "Mary Harris Jones." National Women's History Museum, 2015. https://www.womenshistory .org/education-resources/biographies/mary-harris-jones.

Mother Jones Museum. "Who Was Mother Jones?" Accessed May 28, 2019. http://www.motherjonesmuseum .org/information/who-was-mother-jones/.

Muir, John. *The Story of My Boyhood and Youth*. New York: Houghton Mifflin Company, 1913.

Nobel Media. "Albert Einstein—Biographical." The Nobel Prize. Accessed May 25, 2019. https://www.nobelprize.org/prizes/physics/1921 /einstein/biographical/.

Olympic Channel. "The Story of Nadia Comaneci, Gymnastics' Perfect 10 Icon | Legends Live On." YouTube video, 26:03. Posted December 26, 2017. https:// www.youtube.com/watch?v=3jReR9pL4Nw.

Padavick, Robert, and Iman Abdulmajid. "An Intimate Interview with Supermodel and Activist Iman." Enough Project, March 8, 2010. http://dev.enoughproject.org /category/celebrity/iman.

Panek, Richard. "The Year of Albert Einstein." Smithsonian Institution, June 1, 2005. https://www.smith sonianmag.com/science-nature/the-year-of-albert -einstein-75841381/.

Pei Cobb Freed & Partners. "I. M. Pei." Accessed June 1, 2019. https://www.pcf-p.com/about/i-m-pei/.

Resendes, Mary Ann. "Muir Family Stories." Central Sierra Historical Society, March 5, 2002. https:// sierrahistorical.org/muir-family-stories/.

Rolling Stone. "100 Greatest Guitarists." *Rolling Stone*, December 18, 2015. https://www.rollingstone.com

/music/music-lists/100-greatest-guitarists-153675
/carlos-santana-2-156054/.

Rubenstein, David, and Madeleine Albright. "The
Life and Career Of Madeleine Albright." C-Span.
Washington, DC, September 7, 2016.

Samorzik, Elad. "Mikhail Baryshnikov Dances His Way
to Tel Aviv." *Haaretz*, November 4, 2011. https://www
.haaretz.com/1.5206482.

Santana (website). "Carlos Santana Biography."
Accessed June 6, 2019. https://www.santana.com
/carlos-santana-biography/.

Sapienza, Terry. "I. M. Pei, Preeminent Architect of Civic
Centers and Cultural Institutions, Dies at 102."
The Washington Post, May 16, 2019. https://www
.washingtonpost.com/local/obituaries/im-pei
-preeminent-architect-of-civic-centers-and-cultural
-institutions-dies-at-102/2019/05/16/f8e71e5a-7820
-11e9-bd25-c989555e7766_story.html?noredirect
=on&utm_term=.d08e927363ab.

Smith, Sam. "Mutombo's Tale Wags Happily." *The Chicago
Tribune*, May 6, 1997. https://www.chicagotribune.com
/news/ct-xpm-1997-05-06-9705060379-story.html.

U.S. Department of State. "Biographies of the Secretar-
ies of State: Madeleine Korbel Albright (1937–)." Office
of the Historian. Accessed May 27, 2019. https://

history.state.gov/departmenthistory/people/albright -madeleine-korbel.

U.S. Department of the Interior. "Dr. Mabel Ping-Hua Lee." National Park Service. Last modified April 19, 2019. https://www.nps.gov/people/mabel-lee.htm.

U.S. Department of the Interior. "John Muir." National Park Service. Last modified May 13, 2018. https://www .nps.gov/yose/learn/historyculture/muir.htm.

U.S. Department of the Interior. "Theodore Roosevelt and Conservation." National Park Service. Last modified November 16, 2017. https://www.nps.gov/thro/learn /historyculture/theodore-roosevelt-and-conservation .htm.

Waldrop, Mitch. "Inside Einstein's Love Affair with 'Lina'—His Cherished Violin." *National Geographic*, February 3, 2017. https://news.nationalgeographic .com/2017/02/einstein-genius-violin-music-physics -science/.

Wiesel, Elie. *Night*. New York: Hill & Wang, 1958.

Wood, Harold. "Was John Muir a Draft Dodger?" Sierra Club. Accessed July 5, 2019. https://vault.sierraclub.org /john_muir_exhibit/life/was_john_muir_a_draft _dodger.aspx.

Quotation Sources

Levi Strauss
Panek, Tracey. "What 9-Year-Olds Want to Know About Levi Strauss." Levi Strauss & Co. May 25, 2016. https://www.levistrauss.com/2016/02/25/what-9-year-olds-want-to-know-about-levi-strauss/.

Mary Harris Jones
Jones, Mary Harris. *Autobiography of Mother Jones*. Chicago: Charles H. Kerr, 1925.

John Muir
Muir, John. *Steep Trails: California, Utah, Nevada, Washington, Oregon, Grand Canyon*. Boston: Houghton Mifflin, 1918.

Albert Einstein
Viereck, George Sylvester. "What Life Means to Einstein." *Saturday Evening Post*, October 26, 1929.

Mabel Ping-Hua Lee
Lee, Mabel. "The Meaning of Woman Suffrage." *The Chinese Student Monthly*, May 1914.

Maya Deren
Deren, Maya. "The Artist as a God in Haiti." *The Tiger's Eye*. December 1948.

I. M. Pei
Ouroussoff, Nicolas. "For I. M. Pei, History Is Still Happening." *The New York Times*, December 12, 2008. https://www.nytimes.com/2008/12/14/arts/design /14ouro.html.

Elie Wiesel
Wiesel, Elie. "Hope, Despair, and Memory." Nobel Lecture, December 11, 1986. https://www.nobelprize.org /prizes/peace/1986/wiesel/lecture/.

Madeleine Albright
Albright, Madeleine. "The Promise of Peace." Tufts Lecture Series, 2007 Issam M. Fares Lecture. http:// www.issamfares.org/en/Subpage.aspx?pageid=1741.

Isabel Allende
Isabel Allende Foundation. "Isabel Allende Foundation Announces Espíritu Awards." October 22, 2002. https:// www.isabelallende.org/docs/press_release_2002.pdf? Rjx11jpcx.

Carlos Santana
Heath, Chris. "The Epic Life of Carlos Santana." *Rolling Stone*, March 16, 2000. https://www.rollingstone.com /music/music-news/the-epic-life-of-carlos-santana -89485/.

Mikhail Baryshnikov

Isenberg, Barbara. "To Mikhail Baryshnikov, Time Is a Great Teacher." *Los Angeles Times*, August 30, 2009. https://www.latimes.com/entertainment/arts/la-ca-baryshnikov30-2009aug30-story.html.

Iman Abdulmajid

Lauder, Aerin, and Iman Abdulmajid. "Women We Love: Iman." Estée Lauder. Accessed July 1, 2019. https://www.esteelauder.com/estee-stories-article-secret-my-success-iman.

Nadia Comăneci

Ciruca, Vlad, and Nadia Comăneci. "Olympic Gymnast Nadia Comăneci Gives Advice to Startups." Whiteboard. Accessed July 1, 2019. http://www.whiteboardmag.com/nadia-Comaneci/.

Dikembe Mutombo

Joseph, Adi. "Dikembe Mutombo Reveals His Secret to Success." *USA Today*, August 17, 2017. https://www.usatoday.com/story/sports/ftw/2017/08/17/dikembe-mutombo-reveals-his-secret-to-success/104677780/.

About the Author

Brooke Khan holds a secondary teaching credential in Language Arts and Social Science as well as a master's degree in Education. After spending over a decade teaching history, language arts, and reading at the high school and middle school level, she left the classroom to start her own business, Literacy in Focus LLC, where she creates and publishes engaging materials for teachers all over the world. Her differentiated curriculum is designed to support educators in using content to build literacy. Brooke lives in Southern California with her husband and son. She enjoys reading, traveling, and spending time outdoors.

CPSIA information can be obtained
at www.ICGtesting.com
Printed in the USA
LVHW070248280320
650987LV00010B/6